SCIENCE ADVENTURERS

CLIMATE SCIENTISTS

BY CAROL HAND

CONTENT CONSULTANT

Atreyee Bhattacharya, PhD
Visiting Researcher, Scripps Institution of Oceanography, University of California, San Diego
Research Affiliate, Institute of Arctic and Alpine Research (INSTAAR), University of Colorado, Boulder

Essential Library
An Imprint of Abdo Publishing
abdobooks.com

ABDOBOOKS.COM

Published by Abdo Publishing, a division of ABDO, PO Box 398166, Minneapolis, Minnesota 55439. Copyright © 2020 by Abdo Consulting Group, Inc. International copyrights reserved in all countries. No part of this book may be reproduced in any form without written permission from the publisher. Essential Library™ is a trademark and logo of Abdo Publishing.

Printed in the United States of America, North Mankato, Minnesota.
092019
012020

THIS BOOK CONTAINS RECYCLED MATERIALS

Cover Photos: ANT Photo Library/Science Source (front); Shutterstock Images (back)
Interior Photos: Martin Zwick/REDA&CO/Universal Images Group/Getty Images, 4–5; D.A. Peel/Science Source, 8, 11; Jim West/Science Source, 12; Lisa McKeon/Northern Rocky Mountain Science Center-BRD/USGS, 14–15; USGS/Science Source, 17; USGS, 19; Alex Brylov/Shutterstock Images, 23; iStockphoto, 24–25, 52, 59, 68–69, 73, 74–75; Evan Oto/Science Source, 29; Pixel Jazz Productions/Shutterstock Images, 30; Dionys Moser/McPhoto/ullstein bild/Getty Images, 32–33; Red Line Editorial, 35; Adrian Wojcik/iStockphoto, 36–37; Mark Ralston/AFP/Getty Images, 38; Luis Sinco/Los Angeles Times/Getty Images, 41; NASA Earth Observatory/Landsat/USGS/Science Source, 42–43; Vadim Nefedov/iStockphoto, 46–47; Igor Batenev/Shutterstock Images, 50; Andrew Peacock/iStockphoto, 55; Shutterstock Images, 56–57; Matthew J Thomas/Shutterstock Images, 60–61; Ashley Cooper/Corbis Historical/Getty Images, 63; NOAA Corps, Lt. Elizabeth Crapo/AP Images, 65; Alastair Grant/AP Images, 66; GLF Media/Shutterstock Images, 70; NASA/AP Images, 77; Rainer von Brandis/iStockphoto, 80–81; Philippe Psaila/Science Source, 83; European Space Agency/Science Source, 84–85; NASA/Science Source, 88; Kim Shiflett/KSC/NASA, 91; Matt Mazloff/Science Source, 92–93; NASA/Goddard Institute for Space Studies/Science Source, 97; Thierry Berrod/Mona Lisa Production/Science Source, 98–99

Editor: Melissa York
Series Designer: Laura Graphenteen

LIBRARY OF CONGRESS CONTROL NUMBER: 2019942027

PUBLISHER'S CATALOGING-IN-PUBLICATION DATA

Names: Hand, Carol, author.
Title: Climate scientists / by Carol Hand
Description: Minneapolis, Minnesota : Abdo Publishing, 2020 | Series: Science adventurers | Includes online resources and index.
Identifiers: ISBN 9781532190339 (lib. bdg.) | ISBN 9781532176180 (ebook)
Subjects: LCSH: Climatology--Juvenile literature. | Climatic changes--Juvenile literature. | Scientists--Juvenile literature. | Discovery and exploration--Juvenile literature. | Adventure and adventurers--Juvenile literature.
Classification: DDC 551.6--dc23

CONTENTS

CHAPTER ONE
ICE CORES AND CLIMATE CHANGE 4

CHAPTER TWO
MELTING GLACIERS 14

CHAPTER THREE
CARBON DIOXIDE 24

CHAPTER FOUR
MELTING PERMAFROST 36

CHAPTER FIVE
AT THE POLES 46

CHAPTER SIX
RISING SEA LEVELS 60

CHAPTER SEVEN
OCEAN CHEMISTRY 74

CHAPTER EIGHT
USING SATELLITE DATA 84

CHAPTER NINE
CLIMATE MODELING TODAY AND TOMORROW 92

ESSENTIAL FACTS	100	SOURCE NOTES	106
GLOSSARY	102	INDEX	110
ADDITIONAL RESOURCES	104	ABOUT THE AUTHOR	112

CHAPTER ONE
ICE CORES AND CLIMATE CHANGE

It's midnight on the fourth of July in the middle of Greenland. Drs. Richard Alley, Joan Fitzpatrick, and other members of their scientific team are playing in the midnight sun, "two miles vertically from the nearest rock," says Alley.[1] In other words, they are standing on an ice sheet two miles (3.2 km) deep. On this holiday, they are chilling out, hitting golf balls and playing volleyball. But the next day they will be back at work, pursuing research on climate change by collecting ice cores. To collect the cores, Alley and Fitzpatrick dig two adjacent snow pits, each about six feet (1.8 m) deep, with a thin wall between them. They place a roof of boards over the pit they are in. Sun shines into the other side, showing the snow layers through the wall, a new layer for each summer and each winter. Those layers, reaching miles

Greenland's vast expanses of ice dwarf the tents of any people who come to camp there.

down all the way to Greenland's land, form the raw data found in ice cores—data that tells the story of past climates.

WHY STUDY ICE CORES?

Ice cores paint a picture of the past—a "two-mile time machine," Alley called it in his book of the same name.[2] Ice cores teach scientists about past temperatures, precipitation levels, volcanic activity, and wind patterns. Ice core layers are similar to tree rings, and it is possible to date an ice core using its layers. They are laid down annually, and summer and winter layers can be distinguished. The topmost, newer layers are thicker and contain the most detailed information, even data about individual seasons or storms. Older, deeper layers are thinner and more compressed, so their information is less detailed and precise.

Analyzing air bubbles trapped in the ice reveals the composition of the atmosphere at the time they were trapped, including the amounts of greenhouse gases such as carbon dioxide and methane. Scientists can compare amounts of these gases during past times to amounts present in today's atmosphere. Since greenhouse gas concentrations are connected to temperature, comparing them shows temperature changes as well. Stable isotopes of oxygen in the ice give even more precise indications of past temperature. As temperatures warm and evaporation increases, more

Over the past 400,000 years, atmospheric carbon dioxide levels ranged from 180 to 280 parts per million (ppm), but they have risen steadily above that range since the Industrial Revolution of the 1700s and 1800s.[3]

of a lighter-weight oxygen isotope and less of a heavier isotope enter the air. Some of the isotopes fall in snow, which is then converted to ice. Scientists use a mass spectrometer to measure isotope concentrations, giving a detailed history of temperature changes through time. Measuring the thickness of annual ice core layers tells scientists about rain and snowfall rates over time. Bubble-free melt layers indicate warmer summer air temperatures, and their locations throughout the ice core layers gives a picture of past climate change.

> "Greenhouse gases really do matter, and we can't make sense of climate history without them."[4]
> —*Richard Alley*

OBTAINING AN ICE CORE

Obtaining an ice core is—not surprisingly—a cold process. Researchers and drillers travel on ski planes over several hundred miles of snow and ice. They live in tents on the ice, where summer temperatures reach -30 degrees Fahrenheit (-34.4°C), bundled in parkas and layers of warm clothing. Aided by computers and skis, snowmobiles and tractors with tracks, they spend the short Arctic summers using drills and muscle power to remove cylindrical cores from the ice sheet below them.

In some cases, scientists can identify the exact year an ice core layer was created based on the materials it contains. For example, in 1783, a huge volcano erupted in Iceland, and volcanic ash settled on Greenland's snow. In 1954, the US military set off a radioactive bomb in the Bikini Atoll, a group of islands in the Pacific. The following year, some of that radioactive dust settled on Greenland's snow. As these materials were buried beneath each

A glaciologist removes an ice core from a drill.

following year's snow, they became markers that scientists now use to check the accuracy of their ice core dates. Ice cores from Greenland date back 130,000 years; some from the Antarctic ice sheet are 800,000 years old.[5]

Ice cores are drilled vertically, sometimes all the way to the bottom of the ice sheet. The core is made in sections, determined by the length of the drill barrel. It's not possible to drill a single core two miles (3.2 km) deep. Typical ice core sections range from approximately three to 20 feet (1 to 6 m) long, and two to five inches (5 to 13 cm) in diameter. Sections are retrieved by lowering the drill, cutting a core section, raising the section to the surface, and then lowering the drill again. Each repeating cycle is called a drill run.

The drillers' job is sometimes uncomfortable or risky. During the Greenland Ice Sheet Project, a drilling tower reached 70 feet (20 m) above the dome that protected the drillers. On windy days, a driller had to climb above the dome and up the tower when the drill was pulled from the hole to remove a core section. The driller wrapped a strap around the drill and held onto it, preventing it from blowing around in the wind and hurting people or getting damaged.

HOW TO DRILL AN ICE CORE

Ice cores are drilled using either mechanical or thermal drills. Both types cut a circle around a central core. A mechanical drill is a rotating pipe or barrel with cutters at the head. When the drill rotates, the cutters cut a circular path through the ice, the core moves up inside the pipe, and the cuttings are removed and sent to a chamber within the drill. Mechanical drills called hand augers are turned by hand. Others are electromechanical, turned by electric motors. Thermal drills lack cutters. Instead, they have heating elements that melt the ice around the pipe. Melt water is stored in a tank inside the drill. Electromechanical drills are used to cut very cold ice; thermal drills are used on warmer ice.

STORING AND HANDLING ICE CORES

Ice cores are flown from their site of origin to one of several facilities where they are stored, studied, and sampled by other scientists. One such facility is the National Science Foundation Ice Core Facility (NSF-ICF). It's located at the Denver Federal Center and operated by the US Geological Survey. NSF-ICF houses almost 56,000 feet (17,000 m) of ice cores collected from Antarctica, Greenland, and North America. Its freezer is 55,000 cubic feet (1,600 cu m) in size and stays at a temperature of -32.8 degrees Fahrenheit (-36°C).[6]

New ice cores arrive in insulated boxes and are left in the main freezer until they reach the freezer's temperature. Cores are unpacked, organized, and placed on racks. They are then entered into the facility's inventory system, where each core is identified so it can be found again based on the date, time, and location of its collection. Next to the main freezer is an exam room where scientists can take out their ice cores. This huge room is held at -13 degrees Fahrenheit (-25°C). Here, scientists cut samples from the ice cores, which they ship back to laboratories for study. Few studies are actually done in the exam room.

DEEP VS. SHALLOW ICE CORES

To drill ice cores from the top 65 to 100 feet (20 to 30 m) of an ice sheet, scientists use a hand auger. Extension rods are added to the auger as drilling goes deeper. The auger is pulled up to retrieve each core section. Drilling below 130 feet (40 m) requires electromechanical or specialized thermal drills. These drills hang on a cable that runs over a top wheel on a vertical tower. Electrical wires in the cable enable people to operate the drill from the surface. This is called cable-suspended drilling. At depths greater than 1,000 feet (300 m), the temperature and pressure of the ice may cause the borehole to close. A drilling fluid prevents this problem by keeping the pressure equal between the ice and the hole.

A tall electromechanical ice drill allows scientists to extract ice from almost 1,000 feet (300 m) below the surface.

Ice cores are kept on many rows of shelves at the NSF-ICF.

Ice core studies illuminate climate history, providing one key piece in understanding how Earth's climate functions. Scientists of all types are looking at climate change from all directions. They are studying ice and permafrost, carbon dioxide in the atmosphere and oceans, rising sea levels, and the effects of climate on animals and plants. They view the whole Earth from satellites and simulate climate in complex computer models. They hope this vast cooperative effort will lead to effective climate change solutions.

THE DRILLER'S LIFE

Drillers build the drilling towers. They fine-tune the drills to keep them running efficiently, wrestle them into place during drill runs, and keep the drilling process operating smoothly and safely. By a project's end, they have used a huge and dangerous machine to produce a massive core often weighing 40 short tons (36 metric tons). Drillers also handle cargo. They might direct a cargo plane into a landing site, dig it out after it sinks in soft snow, remove tons of cargo from the plane by hand to get it moving again, and organize the unloaded cargo before it is buried by the next snowstorm. They might fix broken equipment on the ice, cook for the whole crew, or even organize a party. According to Alley, drillers he has worked with are people who might patent an invention, create a new mountain-climbing route, or build an airplane. Alley says, "They tend to be smart, self-confident, experienced, [and] talented."[7]

CHAPTER TWO

MELTING GLACIERS

Nowhere is climate change more evident than in the melting of glaciers. Daniel Fagre and his colleagues from the US Geological Survey (USGS) have been measuring the melting of glaciers in Montana's Glacier National Park for more than a decade. As they climb the Sperry Glacier, Fagre points out that it is now a much longer trek to reach the glacier because so much ice has melted. In 1901, the glacier covered more than 800 acres (320 hectares), but by 2019, it covered less than 250 acres (100 ha).[1] Muir Glacier in Alaska is another dramatic example of melting. Between 1941 and 2004, the edge of the glacier moved back seven miles (11.3 km), and its thickness decreased by more than 2,625 feet (800 m).[2]

Glaciers form when snowfall during a year exceeds snowmelt. Glaciers retreat, or decrease in size, when snowmelt is greater than snowfall. As the average global temperature increases, glaciers around the world are

At Grinnell Glacier in Glacier National Park, a USGS scientist sets up a camera that will take repeated images to document the glacier's shrinking.

"Things that normally happen in geologic time are happening during the span of a human lifetime. It's like watching the Statue of Liberty melt."[5]
—*Daniel Fagre, USGS*

A GLACIER IS GROWING. IS MELTING OVER?

Greenland's Jacobshavn Glacier, the island's largest glacier, has thickened slightly around its edges since 2016. This is happening because of a recent influx of colder water from the North Atlantic. The Jacobshavn Glacier drains only 7 percent of the Greenland ice sheet. Although this small part of the ice sheet is growing, this growth is far outweighed by rapid melting of the other 93 percent of Greenland's ice. According to Josh Willis, a NASA oceanographer and head of the Oceans Melting Greenland (OMG) project, other Arctic glaciers may be undergoing similar growth. Melting is complicated and not a straight-line process, he says. It is highly dependent on ocean temperatures, which ebb and flow, with warm and cold temperatures alternating in a natural cycle about every 20 years. Still, although melting slows every 20 years, the trend is definitely toward a melting of the Greenland ice sheet.[6]

retreating. Glaciers are a small but important portion of the total water on Earth. Only 3.5 percent of Earth's water is freshwater; about 70 percent of that is the ice of glaciers and ice sheets.[3] Glaciers in Glacier National Park have existed for at least 7,000 years, probably longer.[4] Some increased significantly in size during the Little Ice Age, a time of cooling between the years 1400 and 1850 that was cold, but less intense than a true ice age. Glaciers are vital to Earth's ecology. In late summer, cold glacial meltwater provides many human communities with water for drinking, farming, and recreation. Fish and aquatic insect species depend on the meltwater too.

WHEN GLACIERS MELT

Glaciers' retreat has an impact beyond the newly exposed land at their margins. As the land-based meltwater runs into the oceans and raises sea levels, oceans rise and flood small islands and continental shores. Some coral reefs will die as they are covered by deeper water and receive too little sunlight. Below melting glaciers, flooding will increase. Then as the glaciers disappear, there will be a shortage of freshwater. Farm production will decline, and hydroelectric power plants will produce less energy. Animals will lose habitats and food sources, and old pollutants that were trapped in glaciers will be released. Glaciers are still in the early stages of retreat. They cover almost 10 percent of Earth's land surface and still provide Earth's largest reservoir of freshwater.[7]

Patrick Gonzalez is a principal climate change scientist with the National Park Service. Gonzalez conducts research on how climate change is affecting national parks. He studies how ecosystems can reduce climate change by storing carbon. National parks are good areas for

Scientists set up stakes on Sperry Glacier in Glacier National Park to monitor changing snow levels.

studying climate change because they have been protected from other factors, such as deforestation, farming, and city growth.

Gonzalez looks for statistically significant changes in the parks' characteristics over time, analyzing causes of these changes. One obvious change is in the size of glaciers, or the amount of snow they contain. Gonzalez and his colleagues across the country measure both the area of the glacier and its depth. Changing depth can be measured simply by planting a stake or pole and measuring the part of the stake that is visible in succeeding years. These measurements show that the snowpack is at its lowest level in the last 800 years. Tidal gauges along shores show sea levels rising between 6.7 and 8.3 inches (17 and 21 cm) during the 1900s.[8]

GLACIER NATIONAL PARK

Most of America's glaciers are confined to the tallest mountain peaks, which are located in US national parks. These include one park in Montana, two in Alaska, and two in Washington State. During the past century, park visitors have watched as US glaciers—slowly at first and now increasingly rapidly—melt into water and run off into the nation's rivers and out to sea.

Montana's Glacier National Park receives the most attention because its glaciers are melting rapidly. In 1850, the area had 150 glaciers of 25 acres (10 ha) or larger; today, due to climate change, there are only 25, and by 2030, there may be none.[9] The USGS analyzes

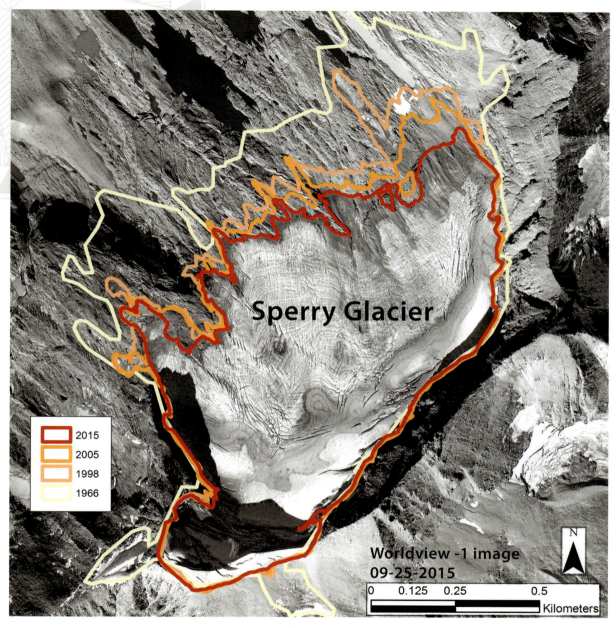

Sperry Glacier in Glacier National Park continues to retreat.

glacier areas using aerial photography and, more recently, satellite images. By capturing glaciers from the same position in different years, these images can show how the glaciers have changed. A series of images from 1966, 1998, 2005, and 2015/2016 show the changing perimeters of these glaciers over 50 years. All glaciers have decreased in area, some by as much as 85 percent. On average, the total glacier area has been reduced by about 39 percent.[10]

OTHER US GLACIERS

Alaska's Glacier Bay National Park has seven huge tidewater glaciers. These unusual glaciers have flowed down mountains, eventually reaching sea level. Wrangell Saint Elias National Park and Preserve is the country's largest national park, covering 13.2 million acres (5.3 million ha). It contains 5,000 square miles (12,950 sq km) of glaciers, including some of the world's largest.[12] Washington State's Mount Rainier, in Mount Rainier National Park, has more glaciers on its slopes than any other mountain in the lower 48 states. Meltwater from its largest, the Emmons Glacier, feeds six rivers. The peaks of North Cascades National Park have over 300 glaciers.[13]

MELTING WORLDWIDE

Most European glaciers are in the Alps. Switzerland has 1,500 glaciers, and it gets 60 percent of its power from hydroelectric dams, many fed by glacial meltwater.[11] Swiss Alpine glaciers are melting faster than the global average; since 2001, they have retreated every year. For the next few decades, as meltwater increases, hydroelectric power generation will be more efficient. But as glaciers continue their retreat, meltwater and power generation will decrease. Researchers hope hydropower can continue by using stored rainwater. Robert Boes is the director of the Laboratory of Hydraulics, Hydrology and Glaciology at the Swiss Federal Institute of Technology. His institute's researchers are using radar to study the bedrock underlying present-day glaciers.

This will uncover the region's future topography, including the location of valleys once covered by ice that may become potential water storage reservoirs.

In Peru, Bolivia, and Colombia, glaciers high in the Andes rise above tropical ecosystems, supplying water for at least 19 million people in the valleys below.[14] According to Bryan Mark, a glaciologist from Ohio State University, most Andean glaciers could melt by 2040. Penn State University professor Karl Zimmerer studies the effects of climate change on the diversity of agricultural species and food security. He and his colleagues develop computer models showing relationships between humans and agricultural ecosystems in tropical regions of South America. He applies possible climate-change impacts to his models to determine how likely these food systems are to adapt to change. His goal is to make food production more sustainable. Zimmerer also promotes new technology to help farmers share information about the availability of seeds and other resources. Such regional connections, he says, could help the people who live there share resources and lessen food shortages.

GLACIERS AT THE ROOF OF THE WORLD

Asia's Himalayan glaciers are also imperiled. An April 2019 study states that more than one-third of Himalayan glaciers may melt before 2100, directly threatening the water supply of 240 million people.[15] This region, called the Hindu Kush Himalayan (HKH) region, includes some of the world's tallest mountains, including Mount Everest. It feeds ten of the world's most important river systems, including the Ganges and Indus. Directly or indirectly, water from these glaciers supplies food, energy, clean air, and income for almost two billion people.[16] The rate at which the HKH glaciers will melt depends on the rate of global warming. Temperatures rise faster in mountains than in valleys, and as the ice melts, the melt rate increases even faster because the newly uncovered dark earth absorbs heat instead of reflecting it as ice does.

> "Glaciers are sentinels of climate change. They are the most visible evidence of global warming today."[17]
>
> —*James Balog, founder of Extreme Ice Survey, a huge photographic survey of changing glaciers*

Melting glaciers around the world will result in increased short-term flooding and long-term water shortages downstream. They will harm several billion people by lowering water supplies and making farms less productive. Glaciers are land-based, so as they melt and flow into the oceans, they contribute to sea-level rise. Thus, people along the world's coasts, even those who have never seen a glacier, will be affected by glacial melting.

Melting mountain glaciers affect communities around the world.

CHAPTER THREE
CARBON DIOXIDE

Since 1970, the rate at which Earth's temperature is rising has nearly doubled, thanks to the effects of greenhouse gases released by human activity. These gases include carbon dioxide, methane, and nitrous oxide, all of which are at their highest levels in the atmosphere in the past 800,000 years.[1] The most abundant greenhouse gas is carbon dioxide. Much of the sunlight that warms Earth is absorbed at Earth's surface and radiated back into the atmosphere as heat. Greenhouse gases capture and absorb much of this reflected heat, radiating it back down to Earth's surface or to another greenhouse gas molecule. The heat captured and absorbed by greenhouse gases keeps Earth warm enough to support life. The rest of the heat radiates back out to space.

This natural process by which greenhouse gases keep the planet warm is called the greenhouse effect. Without greenhouse gases, too much of

Burning fossil fuels in vehicles is one way humans release carbon dioxide into the atmosphere.

the heat reflected from Earth's surface would be lost into space, and the planet would quickly become too cold to support life. Earth's average annual temperature is almost 60 degrees Fahrenheit (15.6°C); without the greenhouse effect, it would be below freezing and life would not exist.[2] Greenhouse gases are always present in very tiny concentrations, low enough to measure in parts per million (ppm) or even parts per billion (ppb). For comparison, one percent equals one part per hundred. Greenhouse gases are considered trace gases. Altogether, they account for about one-tenth of one percent of atmospheric gases.

TOO MUCH, TOO LITTLE, JUST RIGHT

The strength of a planet's greenhouse effect helps determine its temperature. Venus's atmosphere is nearly all carbon dioxide; it has about 154,000 times as much of the gas in its atmosphere as Earth does.[3] Venus has a runaway greenhouse effect—its surface temperature is hot enough to melt lead. Mars's atmosphere is also mostly carbon dioxide. But its atmosphere is extremely thin and lacks water vapor and methane. Its greenhouse effect is extremely weak, making it a barren, frozen planet. Earth, between the two, has an atmosphere thick enough to retain carbon dioxide and other greenhouse gases, and its temperature is just right to support life.

HOW CARBON DIOXIDE RELATES TO TEMPERATURE

Until the Industrial Revolution in the 1700s and 1800s, the concentration of greenhouse gases in the atmosphere remained relatively stable for hundreds of thousands of years, and so did the global temperature. During the past 800,000 years, levels of carbon dioxide in the atmosphere never rose above 300 ppm, although they cycled from lows during ice ages to highs during interglacial periods. Only when humans began adding carbon dioxide by burning fossil fuels did atmospheric levels began to rise, along with global temperatures. The carbon in fossil fuels has been stored underground for millions of years. But as humans burn coal, oil, and gas, it is being returned to the atmosphere in only a few hundred years. In 2017, carbon dioxide concentrations reached 405 ppm for the first time in three million years. At that time, global temperatures were 3.6 to 5.4 degrees Fahrenheit (2 to 3°C) higher than temperatures during the pre-industrial era.[4]

Atmospheric concentrations of carbon dioxide have risen significantly since humans began burning fossil fuels. Deforestation also contributes to carbon dioxide increase, since the cut forests can no longer take up the gas. And because atmospheric carbon dioxide traps heat, the temperature of Earth and its atmosphere rise as carbon dioxide rises.

THE KEELING CURVE

The best modern record of changes in atmospheric carbon dioxide began in 1958, when Caltech postdoctoral student Charles David Keeling installed

> "Increases in greenhouse gases have tipped the Earth's energy budget out of balance, trapping additional heat and raising Earth's average temperature."[5]
> —Rebecca Lindsey, climate.gov

REAL-WORLD CARBON DIOXIDE CHANGES

Scientists are monitoring exact changes in levels of carbon dioxide and other greenhouse gases. But Eugene Brower sees these changes in his everyday life. Brower is a member of the Inupiat Community who lives in Barrow, Alaska. His family's ice cellars are dug into ground that was once frozen year-round, but they are now melting, causing his stores of whale skin and blubber to spoil. The floors of a local school building rise and fall like the floors of a funhouse because the rapidly melting permafrost beneath has caused the foundation to buckle. Erosion threatens the town's infrastructure, and disappearing sea ice threatens animal life and Inupiat hunting. Climate change is real and present in the Arctic.

infrared gas analyzers at Mauna Loa Observatory in Hawaii. The gas analyzers provided very precise measurements, and the air above the observatory was remote from cities, forests, and other sources of carbon dioxide, providing very consistent day-by-day readings. Two trends quickly became obvious at Mauna Loa. First, there is a seasonal see-saw pattern, as plants take up carbon dioxide during the spring and summer but stop during the fall and winter. Second, the levels have been steadily rising, due primarily to humans burning fossil fuels.

The Keeling curve is considered the best evidence available of human impact on Earth's processes. The curve shows a very clear relationship between carbon dioxide concentration and fossil fuel burning. Countries and industries release records of the amount of fossil fuels they burn each year, and scientists use the data to calculate how much carbon dioxide is produced by this burning. This provides a rough estimate of carbon dioxide production by fossil fuel emissions. More precise values are obtained by measuring carbon isotopes in the atmosphere. Fifty-seven percent of fossil fuel emissions remain in the atmosphere, and this amount tracks exactly with carbon dioxide concentrations.[6] Marine chemist Andrew Dickson of the Scripps Institute of Oceanography says the oceans have absorbed 30 percent of all carbon dioxide ever produced by humans, and they continue to absorb more.[7]

When Charles Keeling began to measure carbon dioxide concentrations on Mauna Loa, he discovered that the planet behaves with surprising regularity, but that the regularity can only be seen if the measurements are highly accurate.

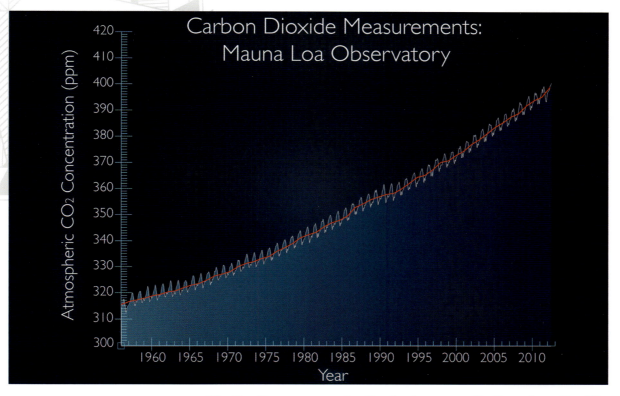

The Keeling curve tracks the rise in atmospheric carbon dioxide.

COLLECTING CARBON DIOXIDE DATA

Long time-series investigations are a vital type of research for climate change. Data collected over many years shows long-term changes in the air and oceans. Two such time-series investigations are taking place in the Sargasso Sea, near Bermuda. The first, Hydrostation S, was established in 1954 by Henry M. Stommel. This station is moored in deep water and has sensors that study currents and air-ocean gas exchange, including carbon dioxide exchange. Scientists visit the station biweekly to collect data. They have

Sea turtles come to dine on the plentiful seaweed in the calm Sargasso Sea.

accumulated the world's longest time-series of this type of data. The second, the Bermuda Atlantic Time-series Study (BATS) station, monitors temperature, chemical composition (including carbon dioxide), and salt levels in deep-ocean water. Data for this study is collected from research vessels that cruise over a much wider range of the ocean than Hydrostation S.

According to Nicholas Bates, a principal investigator for the project, carbon dioxide levels deep in the ocean are rising twice as fast as levels at the surface. Scientists don't know why, but Bates thinks it indicates that something fundamental has changed in the oceans.

At the same time, scientists and citizen scientists are monitoring atmospheric carbon dioxide in different locations around the world. Two locations are Vestmannaeyjar in Iceland and Assekrem in Algeria. Every week, the person collecting data opens a telescoping 15-foot (4.5-m) rod, flips a switch, and activates a computer that fills two 0.6 gallon (2.5 L) flasks with air.[8]

The air from all locations is sent to NOAA's Climate Monitoring and Diagnostics Laboratory in Boulder, Colorado. Under the direction of atmospheric

WALLACE BROECKER, FATHER OF GLOBAL WARMING

Wallace Broecker, a longtime professor at Columbia University, died in February 2019 at age 87. Broecker popularized the term *global warming* in a 1975 scientific article that associated the rise in atmospheric carbon dioxide with warming global temperatures. In 1987, he wrote a classic paper called "The Great Ocean Conveyor," in which he described the ocean's circulation system. He emphasized the interconnectedness of all oceans and the role of their currents in transferring heat around Earth. Broecker was the first to warn that the ocean conveyor belt would be affected by rising atmospheric carbon dioxide levels. He told Congress that a bold new effort was needed to understand these global changes.

scientist Pieter Tans, its chemical composition and concentration of carbon dioxide is analyzed. Like the Keeling curve, these air samples show a continually rising level of atmospheric carbon dioxide. Tans shows a graph with three lines illustrating concentrations of carbon dioxide, methane, and nitrous oxide for the past 1,000 years. Although the concentrations are different, all three follow the same trend for this time period: flat until the mid-1800s, then an upward trend, and after 1950, a much steeper upward trend. This graph, Tans says, shows the effect of humans on greenhouse gas levels.

Beginning with Keeling in the late 1950s and continuing into the present, scientists are monitoring the concentrations of greenhouse gases in the air, and now in the oceans as well. These ongoing data sets provide a baseline to analyze weather and climate changes now and into the future.

Assekrem is the second-highest point in Algeria's Hoggar Mountains, a homeland of the nomadic Tuareg people.

SCIENCE CONNECTION
GREENHOUSE GASES

While overall amounts and percentages of greenhouse gases may be tiny, increases can drastically change Earth's climatic processes—say, from an ice age to a tropical climate. Two features of greenhouse gases determine how they affect climate. One is global warming potential (GWP), or how much a unit of the gas affects warming over a given time period. Carbon dioxide is assigned a GWP of 1. A high-GWP gas causes more warming than a low one. The second feature is atmospheric residence time, or how long the gas stays in the environment before it is broken down chemically. If GWPs are equal, a gas with a long atmospheric lifetime causes more warming than one with a short lifetime.

Because carbon dioxide is by far the most abundant greenhouse gas in the atmosphere, it has the greatest effect on warming. But the other two major gases, methane and nitrous oxide, have significant effects as well, because their GWPs are much higher. That is, a single molecule of methane or nitrous oxide causes much more heating than a single molecule of carbon dioxide. This factor is becoming more important as methane concentrations rise.

*Individual carbon dioxide molecules are in constant flux between reservoirs such as air and ocean, but the overall atmospheric carbon dioxide concentration is quite stable. A given amount lasts about 100 years, some as much as 1,000 years.
**Most recent year of data available is 2014.

GREENHOUSE GAS	CHEMICAL FORMULA	GWP	ATMOSPHERIC RESIDENCE TIME (YEARS)	CONCENTRATION (PPB), SPRING 2019
CARBON DIOXIDE[9]	CO_2	1	100*	414,720
METHANE[10]	CH_4	25	12	1,866
NITROUS OXIDE[11]	N_2O	298	114	331
CHLOROFLUOROCARBON-12 (CFC-12)	CCl_2F_2	10,900	100	0.527**
HYDROFLUOROCARBON-23 (HFC-23)	CHF_3	14,800	270	0.024**
SULFUR HEXAFLUORIDE	SF_6	22,800	3,200	0.0073**
NITROGEN TRIFLUORIDE[12]	NF_3	17,200	740	0.00086**

CHAPTER FOUR
MELTING PERMAFROST

In the Arctic, it stays so cold that, even during the summer, melting only occurs in the top few inches of soil. During the short Arctic summers, plants grow in the few inches of thawed surface soil. Below that is permafrost, or permanently frozen soil. Or at least, that has been the case until recently. World temperatures are rising, and since the 1970s, permafrost has thawed in many places. Technically, permafrost is defined as soil that has been frozen year-round for at least two years. It makes up 24 percent of the land in the Northern Hemisphere and a smaller portion in the Southern Hemisphere.[1] The upper layer, the part that thaws in summer, is called the active layer. As the world warms, the active layer is getting thicker because more soil is melting.

In the short term, melting permafrost can disrupt the surface features above it. The land above melting permafrost melts or changes shape. This

Animals such as the Arctic hare live on the tundra that overlays permafrost.

Erosion caused by melting permafrost and sea ice loss threatens a Yupik village in Alaska.

shifts the foundations of buildings and infrastructure, including roads, pipelines, and airports. Even the trees, used to growing into frozen soil, begin to lean as their once-stable support system buckles. Melting permafrost also releases carbon in the form of methane. This sets in motion a positive feedback loop—that is, warming leads to more warming. Present-day warming releases the methane, and the released methane then further speeds up warming.

Much of the data on permafrost melting in Alaska comes from temperature measurements taken in hundreds of boreholes scattered across the landscape. The boreholes are drilled, then protected by metal caps. They generally range from about 150 to 200 feet (45 to 60 m) deep. The network of boreholes was first established in the early 1980s by Tom Osterkamp. In two boreholes near Barrow, on Alaska's northern coast, the temperature at about 50 feet (15 m) deep rose about 0.9 degrees Fahrenheit (0.5°C) in a decade, according to William Cable of the University of Alaska Fairbanks Geophysical Institute.[2] This corresponds to the temperature rise during the same time period.

POSITIVE FEEDBACK

Factors such as solar radiation and greenhouse gases drive climate change. Feedback is a process that either increases or decreases the effects of these factors. Feedback can be either positive or negative. A negative feedback loop decreases a warming trend, and a positive feedback loop increases it. With melting permafrost, positive feedback occurs when melting releases methane or carbon dioxide. The permafrost originally melts because of warming temperatures. The melting releases more greenhouse gases, which increase the temperature further and cause more rapid melting—a positive feedback loop.

METHANE BUBBLES

Katey M. Walter Anthony stands on a thin area of ice around a thawed pool in a frozen lake near Fairbanks, Alaska. Bubbles come up and burst, one after another, at the surface. The bubbles appear as plant matter and other organic material that was long submerged, often for thousands of years, is unfreezing and now decaying under the water. She bends carefully over this methane "hot spot" and dunks a bottle into the water, collecting a sample for analysis. When studying Siberian lakes in 2000, Walter Anthony discovered that methane does not escape evenly across a lake but instead forms separate large plumes that are most visible in winter after the surface freezes. These plumes meant that probably more methane was being released than scientists had thought. Tests on methane from one of the Alaskan lakes showed that it was 30,000 years old; tests on a Siberian lake put the methane's age at 43,000 years. According to Walter Anthony, "These grasses were food for mammoths during the end of the last ice age. It was in the freezer for 30,000 to 40,000 years, and now the freezer door is open."[3]

When carbon stored in organic material at the lake bottom thaws, it is broken down by bacteria. If there is plenty of oxygen, the decomposed organic matter enters the air as carbon dioxide. But if oxygen is limited, the materials do not break down completely. Instead they enter the air as methane. Most of the release will be carbon dioxide, but methane is so much more powerful that scientists think it will trap as much heat as the carbon dioxide. Walter Anthony is working with Guido Grosse, another scientist at the University of Alaska Fairbanks, to precisely map of the locations

A NEW CARBON SOURCE

Some scientists think the Arctic tundra will change from being a carbon sink (which stores carbon) to a carbon source (which releases it) by the mid-2020s. By 2200, 60 percent of the permafrost in the Northern Hemisphere will probably be melted, releasing about 190 billion short tons (170 billion metric tons) of carbon, or about one-half of all carbon released since the Industrial Revolution. This would have an irreversible effect on the rate of global warming, and slowing it would require a much greater reduction of fossil fuel emissions than is currently planned. In addition, climate change will impact peatlands, which contain 90 percent water and 10 percent partially decomposed plant matter. The highly carbon-rich peat, some of it under the permafrost, is also in danger of melting. A global temperature rise of 1.8 degrees Fahrenheit (1°C) over the next few decades could cause between 38 and 100 million short tons (34 and 89 million metric tons) of carbon per year to be released from peat. This is in addition to the release from thawing permafrost.[4]

Guido Grosse, *right*, pinpoints the location of a methane plume in an Alaskan lake.

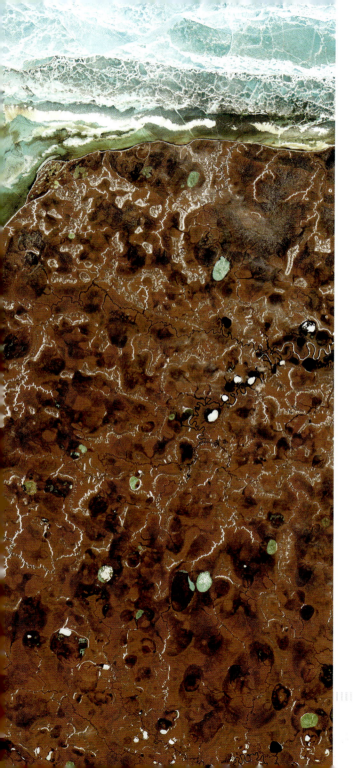

of methane plumes. They also hope to use satellites and aerial photography to detect trends in methane release. These photos will let them see cracks and melting in the ice, as well as the bubbling of methane hot spots.

    Walter Anthony and her colleagues do field studies on frozen lakes. Others study frozen land, collecting data on ground temperature, moisture, and thickness of the active layer. Changes in these factors help them understand how permafrost is changing over time. They make these measurements by drilling holes to different depths and inserting instruments. To overcome the heat created by drilling and prevent the soil from thawing, they use protected pipes and blow cold air into the drill holes. The goal is to disturb the ground as little as possible. They have set up monitoring sites all over the Arctic and maintain them long term. Some sites have been in place since the 1840s, providing valuable historical data that will

A satellite image of Siberia in Russia reveals the lakes and craters that form as permafrost melts.

> "It's a spine-tingling feeling, if it's really old carbon that hasn't been in the air for a long time, and now it's entering the air. That's the fingerprint of a major disruption, and we aren't going to be able to turn it off someday."[6]
> —Edward A. G. Schuur, University of Florida

help in understanding current and future changes in permafrost.

Other scientists study permafrost from space, using satellites. Some satellites circle Earth several times a day and provide information about changes over broad regions. Satellites cannot see the underground permafrost, but they can see landforms that occur only where ground is frozen. They can also measure ground surface temperatures. Some scientists work in laboratories, where they can set up carefully controlled experiments. They can keep soil samples at specific temperatures and measure rates of freezing, thawing, and other changes very precisely. Along with field, lab, and satellite studies, scientists are developing computer models to try to predict future changes in permafrost and how they will affect the climate.

PERMAFROST THREATS

Historically, almost 85 percent of Alaska has been covered with permafrost, but this is changing as global warming proceeds. By 2050, according to a 2018 study in *Nature Communications*, more than four million people and 70 percent of current infrastructure in the Northern Hemisphere will feel negative effects of melting permafrost.[5] In Russia's Ural Mountains, railways and oil pipelines will be damaged even if the world slows greenhouse gas emissions.

Permafrost across the Western Hemisphere is thawing more rapidly, putting existing infrastructure at risk. It is exerting a positive feedback effect on warming in the area. Scientists are just beginning to tackle this serious aspect of climate change. According to the Climate Institute, the future Arctic climate will be warmer, wetter, and more variable.

MELTING SPEEDS UP

Melting Arctic permafrost is releasing carbon dioxide and methane into the atmosphere up to twice as fast as current models predicted. The planet is warming faster and the Arctic landscape is changing faster. A 2019 study described how research sites that were forests a year earlier had become covered with lakes. Once-clear rivers were filled with sediment. Merritt Turetsky of the University of Guelph, Ontario, had measured permafrost temperatures for ten years outside Fairbanks, Alaska. When he returned to his field sites in 2019, all his gauges and equipment were under water. "You can imagine that the electronics did not survive!" he said.[7] Scientists must become more creative to continue doing research in the Arctic. They hope to improve tracking of permafrost regions using drones and lasers and collect more data by increasing the number of observatories and experiments. These changes will require increased funding.

CHAPTER FIVE
AT THE POLES

P olar regions, both the Arctic and the Antarctic, often show the first signs of the impact of climate change on Earth. These fragile systems, balanced at the top and bottom of the world, are vulnerable to feedback processes that magnify tiny atmospheric changes. Ice sheets and sea ice melt rapidly, and the melting exposes darker land and ocean that absorb more heat and further accelerate the rate of heating. The average annual temperature of the Antarctic Peninsula has increased by 5.4 degrees Fahrenheit (3°C) since 1970, and a similar temperature rise has occurred in the Arctic.[1] This has had profound and ongoing effects on the plants and wildlife at both poles, as well as on the human cultures of the Arctic.

The people of Greenland and the rest of the Arctic are feeling the effects of climate change.

POLAR AMPLIFICATION

The Arctic is warming at rates two to three times faster than the rest of the world. This is called polar amplification. This is happening because of positive feedback systems. One system involves melting sea ice. Sea ice is white; it reflects sunlight, which lowers surface temperatures. As sea ice melts, the amount of white surface decreases, and the darker soil and ocean surfaces increase. The darker surfaces absorb heat, speeding up warming. Also, melting permafrost releases methane, further increasing warming. Finally, thunderstorms in the tropics transport heat high into the atmosphere, and global winds move the heat toward higher latitudes. This constant flow of heat from the tropics toward the poles also aids in Arctic amplification.

By 2050, the world population of polar bears may decline by two-thirds, to less than 10,000.[3]

ARCTIC EVOLUTION

Biological evolution is a slow process. According to John J. Wiens of the University of Arizona and his colleague Ignacio Quintero of Yale University, species typically adapt to changing climatic conditions at a rate of about 1.8 degrees Fahrenheit (1°C) per one million years. But global temperatures are predicted to rise by about 7.2 degrees Fahrenheit (4°C) over the next 100 years (according to estimates by the Intergovernmental Panel on Climate Change), and affected species would have to adapt 10,000 times faster than normal to survive. Wiens and Quintero studied the evolutionary histories of 540 species of living organisms to determine typical rates of evolution.[2]

One group of organisms definitely having trouble adapting quickly enough is the polar bear. Until the late 1900s, polar bear numbers were declining due to widespread hunting, but since then, populations have fallen because of rising temperatures. Melting sea ice shrinks polar bear habitat and makes it more difficult for them to hunt seals, their primary prey. Polar bears are highly specialized and unlikely to adapt quickly enough to warming conditions. Some have tried to live on foods from land, but these foods do not provide as much fat as seal meat. Ringed and bearded seal populations are also at risk as the ice melts, further imperiling Arctic food webs.

Dropping reindeer populations on Norway's Svalbard archipelago are strongly linked to climate change. Reindeer spend the entire year in a small area, nibbling on grasses, herbs, and sedges. When it snows, they scratch the snow away with their hooves and keep eating. But warming temperatures lead to more rain and less snow, and the rain freezes to form an ice layer. Reindeer cannot remove the ice to feed, and some starve. In a 2019 study, Norwegian biologist Brage Bremset Hansen and colleagues used data collected since 1994 by other colleagues, who captured and marked baby reindeer every spring, then looked for them again in August. They produced a detailed decades-long picture of reindeer populations of different ages. Hansen and colleagues used this data to create a population model, then used the model to predict how reindeer populations would fare under

STUDYING POLAR BEARS AT THE SOURCE

Kristen Laidre, a principal scientist at the Polar Science Center, University of Washington, studies polar bears in East Greenland. Laidre recently led a study to document the knowledge of native polar bear hunters. Interviewers asked 25 full-time hunters a series of 55 questions, including how hunters navigate their hunting areas, what kinds of environmental changes they are seeing, and how local polar bear populations have changed over the last ten to 15 years.[4] For example, the sea ice has thinned and forms later in the year, so hunters now use boats more than dog sleds, and they are taking sleds out in December rather than October. The hunters also marked maps showing locations of the highest concentrations of polar bears. Learning about polar bears from those who know them best will help scientists assess future populations.

Researchers study a polar bear they have rendered unconscious.

different icing conditions. Under one icy winter, they found that a population crash would occur if reindeer populations were high. But if icy winters were continuous, populations did not crash. The weak had already been killed off, and the remaining populations were smaller, more robust, and less likely to starve. In other words, Hansen found that the reindeer's internal population changes buffered the effects of climate change.

SEA ICE LOSS

Satellites have been tracking sea ice melting since 1979. The ice area has shrunk by about 13.3 percent every decade since. Climate models have predicted a decline for decades, but the actual shrinking is outpacing model estimates. In a 2017 study, Qinghua Ding and his colleagues at the University of California, Santa Barbara, built a complex model including all variables that influence melting of sea ice. When running the model, they turned off, one by one, all the variables related to human-caused global warming. They were left with just the amount of ice melt caused by naturally occurring air currents. They found that air circulation causes 30 to 50 percent of warming.[5] They concluded that human activity is causing ice melting, but natural causes are speeding it up. The Greenland ice sheet is also melting. According to a 2017 United Nations study, the loss of ice from the ice sheet has tripled in two decades.[6] Because this ice is land-based, when it melts and enters the ocean, it raises sea level.

As sea ice declines, some economic activities will ramp up, including shipping, tourism, and oil and gas exploration. However, other changes may cause problems. Changes in the

Climate change may affect everyone in the Arctic who fishes.

location and timing of plankton blooms may alter commercial fisheries. Loss of sea ice and permafrost will increase flooding and erosion and endanger coastal communities. Alaska's 229 recognized Native tribes are already experiencing difficulties. Many depend on fishing and hunting, and as habitats and population sizes of their prey (including polar bears, walruses, seals, fish, and caribou) decline, they must travel longer distances over thinner ice or find alternate food sources.

The Arctic Ocean has lost almost 95 percent of its oldest ice, and it is polluted with toxic algae and the most microplastics of any ocean.[8]

ANTARCTIC CHANGES

Unlike the North Pole, the South Pole has a continent, Antarctica. It is covered by the Antarctic ice sheet. Antarctica can be divided into three regions: East Antarctica, West Antarctica, and the Antarctic Peninsula, which is the smallest and farthest north. The effects of global warming vary across the continent. The size of East Antarctica and the thickness of its ice limit large-scale melting. The temperature in this region is either remaining stable or rising only slightly. However, temperatures in West Antarctica and the Antarctic Peninsula have risen 5.4 degrees Fahrenheit (3°C) since 1970.[7] The only part of Antarctica that is losing a significant amount of ice is the Peninsula.

Simon Morley is a marine ecophysiologist at the British Antarctic Survey in the United Kingdom. Morley and his colleagues published a study in January 2019 that analyzes the likely effects of climate change on 31 groups of Antarctic animals.[9] Morley and his colleagues collected data from studies over the past 40 years and calculated a score for each species or group. The "winners"—those that showed the most positive (or non-negative) impacts—received high scores. Those showing the most negative impacts and the lowest scores were the "losers."

Key losers in Morley's analysis were krill, small, shrimp-like crustaceans that are the base of the food web and a major food source for marine animals in the Antarctic. Krill depend on Antarctic ice for food and shelter, and as the ice melts, their populations plummet. This in turn threatens the species that depend on them. Loss of krill combined with loss of sea ice have led to an 80 percent decline in the number of Adélie penguins in some regions.[10] Emperor and chinstrap penguins are also declining. Gentoo penguins seem to be replacing all of these species. Minke whales and orcas also depend on sea ice, and they appear to be declining around Antarctica. Some species, such as sea stars and sea urchins, will be winners, according to Morley. As the ice decreases, there will be more open sea floor and larger habitats for these species. However, when a key species like krill is lost, it spells serious trouble for the whole ecosystem.

KRILL

Krill feed on algae growing on the bottom of sea ice. As the sea ice declines, the krill decline also. Numbers are hard to estimate, but in the Antarctic, some scientists think krill numbers have dropped as much as 80 percent since 1970.[11] Scientists estimate krill population by tracking sound when it bounces off krill. By determining the properties of the sound compared to the sound of sea water alone, scientists can get a relatively accurate measure of krill numbers. Fish, seals, whales, penguins, and other birds all depend on krill as a food source. Dropping krill numbers means the animals that depend on them will decline or disappear.

Adélie penguins are not broadly endangered, but their numbers are dropping in areas of their range that are feeling the effects of climate change.

Most of Antarctica remains ice bound and stable. But as the climate warms, coastal ice sheets are breaking off and falling into the ocean, particularly on the Antarctic Peninsula. The West Antarctic ice sheet is thinning. About 90 percent of its glaciers are retreating, and the retreat is accelerating.[12] As of 2014, scientists announced that this ice sheet is collapsing. Total collapse may take several hundred years, but the process is thought to be irreversible. As coastal ice sheets melt, pouring water into the ocean, they open the way for inland glaciers to slide toward the sea. As this process begins, it will trigger a positive feedback loop that will accelerate warming.

Changing climate will affect whales and all polar animals.

Scientists from the research ship *Polarstern* set up camp on an ice floe on the Weddell Sea in Antarctica in 2013.

SCIENCE CONNECTION
THE MOSAIC EXPEDITION

How do you learn about climate change when it happens so quickly in one of the most brutal, frozen regions of Earth? Beginning in September 2019, scientists from 17 countries started to find out. These 300 meteorologists, biologists, oceanographers, and ice experts are part of MOSAiC, the Multidisciplinary drifting Observatory for the Study of Arctic Climate. They crewed the RV *Polarstern*, a drifting research station. To complete its mission, it would travel to a remote part of the Siberian Arctic and then cut its engines. The water would freeze around it, and it would stay trapped for a year. The ship hosted about 60 scientists and crew at a time; most scientists planned to stay for two months—assuming the weather allowed ships and aircraft to land.

The scientists spent their time bundled in parkas, wrestling equipment in subzero cold and whiteout conditions. Between December and February, the land plunges into complete darkness. Researchers would collect information on ice, snow, and weather conditions and on the impact of these conditions on Arctic life. They needed to learn how to drill an ice core, identify ice types, ride a snowmobile, and survive a polar bear encounter. According to Melinda Webster, a NASA sea ice expert, the world attempts an expedition of this size, expense, and risk only once in a generation—and, given the speed of climate change, hers might be the last generation that can attempt it.

CHAPTER SIX

RISING SEA LEVELS

One result of rising temperatures and melting ice is sea level rise. Since 1880, average sea level on Earth has risen more than eight inches (23 cm). About three of those eight inches have occurred since 1995. Sea level as of 2019 was rising another 0.13 inches (3.2 mm) per year. During the twenty-first century, oceans will rise between 10 and 30 inches (26 and 77 cm), and air temperatures will rise by 2.7 degrees Fahrenheit (1.5°C), according to the Intergovernmental Panel on Climate Change. A study using data from NASA and European sources predicts a sea level rise of 26 inches (65 cm) by 2100 if current trends continue.[1] This data is a sign of potentially devastating global warming changes in the near future. Sea level rise will damage coastal habitat with erosion and flooding. Salt water will contaminate sources of freshwater. And many plants and animals will lose their habitats. Sea level rise will be accompanied by more rain and more dangerous hurricanes and other storms.

Rising seas can cause shorelines to erode.

MEASURING SEA LEVEL RISE

Getting an accurate measurement of sea level is difficult because so many factors affect it. These include tides, waves, high- and low-pressure areas in the atmosphere, temperature changes, and rain and river water flowing into the oceans. Because these factors are constantly changing, local sea levels are based on mean or average values from readings taken over long time periods.

Scientists often measure local sea level using tide gauges. Modern tide gauges have electronic sensors that continuously record the water level. They send an audio signal down a half-inch (1.3 cm) "sounding tube" and measure how long it takes for the signal to return from the water surface. Data on water level is collected every six minutes, uploaded to a Geostationary Operational Environmental Satellite (GOES), and transmitted directly to the National Oceanographic and Atmospheric Administration (NOAA) headquarters to be analyzed and processed. Tide gauges are usually enclosed in tide houses, attached to the shoreline. The

ART AND CLIMATE

Two Finnish artists, Pekka Niittyvirta and Timo Aho, have installed a piece of art in a Scottish coastal town to show the impact of climate change. The installation, called Lines, consists of three light beams representing a scientific estimate of future sea level rise in a warming Earth. They installed a series of sensors on North Uist, an island community in the Outer Hebrides. The sensors activate the light beams when tides, and therefore water levels, change. The lights cut across the walls of buildings, showing how high rising sea levels will reach. They are mounted on aluminum channels attached either to walls or to steel stems coming out of the ground.

"Climate change movies in general are dramatic and fast and show destruction. . . . But . . . climate change is much more subtle. Like erosion. It takes time, but it's happening."[2]

—*Matthieu Rytz, maker of the film* Anote's Ark, *which tells about rising seas on Kiribati*

electronics are protected inside the house above the water while the sounding tube is outside and submerged in the water.

But sea level does not rise at the same rate everywhere in the world. Two types of measurements are used to determine sea levels in specific areas. Relative sea level, measured by tide gauges, is the height of the water relative to the land. For this measurement to be accurate, researchers must know whether the land itself is moving. They use the Continuous Global Positioning System (CGPS), which monitors vertical movement in the Earth's crust. Satellite altimetry measures the distance between an orbiting satellite and the ocean surface. By knowing the satellite's position, it is possible to tell the ocean's height relative to the center of Earth. Satellite measurements have become extremely accurate.

A tide gauge measures rising sea levels that threaten Tuvalu, a Pacific island nation.

Since 1991, Australian scientists have established a network of monitoring stations on more than ten island countries throughout the South Pacific to measure sea levels. For example, the Marshall Islands station is set up on the main wharf in Uliga. The project is called the Sea Level Fine Resolution Acoustic Measuring Equipment (SEAFRAME). Each station is a typical tide-gauge facility containing sensors that continuously measure water levels; barometric pressure; wind speed, direction, and gusts; and air and water temperatures. These measurements place sea level values in context.

Two other methods of measuring sea level are satellites and drifting buoys. From 1992 until 2005, the TOPEX/POSEIDON (T/P) satellite provided highly accurate measurements of sea level. In 2001, Jason-1 was launched with more advanced instruments. Drifting buoys, also called Argo floats, are robotic sensors. They measure ocean properties (temperature, salt levels, and the speed of ocean currents) at different depths, as well as sea surface height. These data contribute to various projects on climate observation and change. One project is the Climate Variability and Predictability Experiment (CLIVAR), which concentrates on the role of oceans in climate change. As of 2019, 3,890 floats were measuring the ocean down to 6,600 feet (2,000 m).[3]

ISLANDS AND SEA LEVEL RISE

Chip Fletcher, a geologist from the University of Hawaii, follows the effects of rising sea levels in the Pacific Islands. He took core samples to study the history of climate change in the Pacific, specifically on the island of Upolu in Western Samoa. From these cores, he was

NOAA scientists launch an Argo float.

Many South Pacific islands face shortages of freshwater due to rising sea levels.

able to describe cycles of sea level rise and fall. He also models the impacts of sea level rise (past, present, and future) on island environments and communities. Government agencies use his work to develop coastal policy and construction guidelines. Fletcher points out that the worst-case scenario for sea level rise used to be about 3.3 feet (1 m). As of 2017, this was considered an intermediate scenario, and a 6.6-foot (2 m) rise is now considered likely.[4] This will cause problems on all Pacific islands, he says, because populations are highest around coastlines and ports. Rising sea levels will increase flooding, erosion, and saltwater contamination. The islands' freshwater supplies will dwindle long before the islands drown.

This is already happening in many places, including the Hawaiian Islands and many smaller Pacific Islands.

In the Solomon Islands, sea level rise is three times the global average, and in 2016, a study reported the loss of five islands there. The islands were small—2.5 to 12 acres (1 to 5 ha)—and consisted of dense tropical vegetation at least 300 years old. Scientists used various techniques to study the coastlines of 33 reef islands and to document their erosion and the eventual disappearance of five of them.[5] They used aerial and satellite imagery, comparing views between 1947 and 2015. They combined this with local traditional knowledge, radiocarbon dating of trees, records of sea levels, and wave models. Wave energy appears to be important in the dramatic erosion of coastlines. In 2017, Australian scientist Patrick Nunn reported a similar situation in Micronesia. Nunn's team conducted coastal surveys, spoke to local people, and studied satellite images for several low-lying islands throughout the surrounding reef. Two larger islands have disappeared in the last century, and six very small islands disappeared between 2007 and 2014.[6] However, Nunn

DISAPPEARING ISLANDS

The website Acciona points out that the world's Small Island Developing States (SIDS) will be the first to suffer from climate change as rising sea levels overwhelm them. These 52 territories have fragile economies based on tourism and lack protection against natural disasters. Acciona lists nine SIDS considered likely to disappear as sea levels rise: Kiribati, the Maldives, Vanuatu, Tuvalu, the Solomon Islands, Samoa, Nauru, Fiji, and the Marshall Islands.

Micronesia comprises 607 small islands in the Pacific Ocean, just north of the equator. Polynesia consists of more than 1,000 islands in the central and south Pacific Ocean. According to Chip Fletcher of the University of Hawaii, these islands are place-based cultures where the land is considered a family member. Moving would destroy a person's culture, family, and identity. But many—perhaps all—of these islands may be flooded by sea-level rise.

says not all low-lying islands are at risk. Islands that are sheltered or have mangroves or lagoons that trap sediment are resilient and may survive sea-level rise. But many populated islands are at risk. In some cases, such as Kiribati, governments are making plans or are already beginning to evacuate their citizens. But where will they go? Countries in the future will be faced with the decision of how many climate refugees they can allow as immigrants—or whether they will allow any at all.

COASTLINES AND SEA LEVEL RISE

Coastal cities around the world are already developing plans to protect themselves from rising sea levels. Jakarta, Indonesia, has a $40 billion project to build a tall seawall to keep back the water.[7] Rotterdam, Netherlands, is fighting flooding and loss of land by building barriers, drainage systems, and various architectural features to hold water.

Pacific islands that are barely above sea level, including those in the Maldives, are threatened by rising oceans.

Giant gates swing closed to protect Rotterdam from storm surges from the North Sea.

Its projects seek to combat flooding and land loss. They include architectural features such as city squares that become temporary ponds. The city's innovative solutions have made it a model for other cities fighting sea level rise.

A 2019 study of sea level rise in California predicts that the devastation it causes by the end of the century will be ten times greater than the worst earthquakes or wildfires. A team of scientists from the USGS developed a model combining the effects of sea level rise with storms, wave action, coastal erosion, beach loss, and other coastal threats. According to the scientists, even small changes in sea level, when combined with all of the other factors, could affect more than 500,000 people and cause $150 billion in property damage by 2100.[8] Sea level rise is one of the most serious effects of climate change. Monitoring this rise and documenting its impact on land, ecosystems, and people will be key to adapting to climate change in the coming years.

FIRST US CLIMATE REFUGEES

In the United States, one community has already had to relocate. Isle de Jean Charles, Louisiana, is home to members of the Biloxi-Chitimacha-Choctaw Indian nation. It is also sinking into the Gulf of Mexico, and in March 2018, officials announced that the community would be resettled to a new location an hour's drive north. The sinking is partly due to rising sea levels and partly due to settling caused when engineers built giant levees after a 1927 flood. The levees held back the river and also stopped the flow of sediment that allowed the island to rebuild itself. No one is sure how long it will take Isle de Jean Charles to sink. It could last for decades, or one large storm could flood it much sooner.

Glacier melt in Greenland leads to rising sea levels.

SCIENCE CONNECTION
WHAT CAUSES SEA LEVEL RISE?

Sea level rise is a key consequence of climate change. But how exactly does it happen? There are two major processes.

First, sea levels rise because of a property of water known as thermal expansion. As water warms, it expands, so the same amount of water occupies more space. Warm seawater has a greater volume and a lower density than cold seawater. As ocean temperatures rise, sea levels will rise too, even if no more water were added.

Second, sea levels rise when ice on land melts and enters the oceans. This ice comes from mountain glaciers and from the ice sheets on Greenland and Antarctica. The mass of land ice in glaciers and ice sheets depends on the balance between snowfall and snowmelt each year. When more snow falls than melts, ice builds up. But when more snow and ice melt than are replaced, the meltwater flows into the oceans. This is happening now, as summer melting increases and winter snowfall decreases. However, only land-based ice causes a rise in sea level. When sea ice in the Arctic melts every spring and summer, there is no change in sea level because the ice is already displacing water.

CHAPTER SEVEN
OCEAN CHEMISTRY

The oceans cover more than 70 percent of Earth's surface and contain 97 percent of its water. They are also an incredible carbon sink; since the beginning of the Industrial Revolution, they have absorbed 525 billion short tons (476 billion metric tons) of atmospheric carbon dioxide. But the oceans cannot solve the problem of excess carbon dioxide in the atmosphere. First, the oceans cannot absorb all of the carbon dioxide that humans produce each year. Second, the absorbed carbon dioxide does not just lie there quietly. It dissolves to form carbonic acid, making ocean water more acidic, or lowering its pH value. Since the beginning of the Industrial Revolution, oceans have become 30 percent more acidic—a level not seen in 300 million years.[1] The fastest-known natural acidification occurred about 55 million years ago and was about ten times slower.[2] Thus, global warming caused by fossil fuel burning has at least two major effects on oceans—it increases

Earth's oceans have long helped prevent the worst effects of rising carbon dioxide levels.

the temperature of ocean water, and it decreases the pH. Both have serious effects on ocean ecosystems.

The temperature rise results in stronger storms, and it causes serious problems for ocean ecosystems. When temperatures rise, corals undergo bleaching, as they expel the algae (called zooxanthellae) that keep them alive. Toxic blooms of algae increase and, as the algae die off, their decomposition uses up the oxygen, leading to the formation of dead zones where all life either dies or moves away. These are areas of hypoxia (very low oxygen) where most life cannot survive. One of the largest is in the Gulf of Mexico along the southern US coast; this dead zone is the size of Connecticut. A model by dead zones expert Gary Shaffer of the University of Copenhagen predicts that dead zone areas around the world could grow tenfold by 2100.[3] Rising temperature also causes changes in the species structure of communities, as typical species die and exotic species invade.

WARM, ACID OCEANS

In the late 2010s, the ocean pH was about 8.1. Numbers below 7.0 on the pH scale are acidic, while numbers above 7.0 are alkaline. Before the Industrial Revolution, the ocean pH was about 8.2, and research indicates that by 2100, it will decline to about 7.75, according to Columbia University professor Taro Takahashi. In other words, oceans will become 150 percent more acidic, or twice as acidic as before the Industrial Revolution.[4] The degree of acidification, says Takahashi, will depend on the amount of carbon dioxide emitted over this century.

"Any increase in dead zones from global warming will last for thousands of years. They will be a permanent fixture [of our oceans]."[5]

—*Gary Shaffer, University of Copenhagen*

MEASURING OCEAN pH

Very small pH changes are significant in measuring ocean acidification. This is why pH monitoring must be

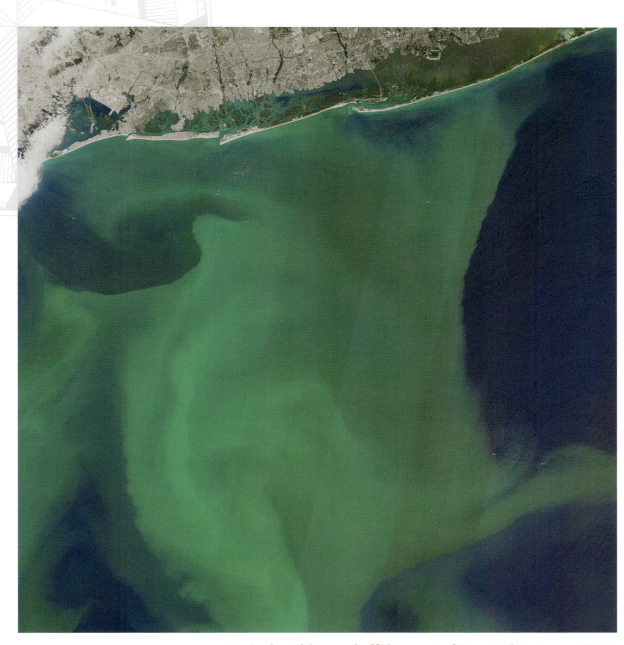

Toxic algae bloomed off the coast of New York in August 2015.

very precise, and measurements must be sensitive and reliable. For measurements before the 1990s, the NOAA National Centers for Environmental Information (NCEI) World Ocean Database uses a large amount of historical pH data. These data are incomplete and vary in reliability. In the early 1990s, Andrew Dickson of the Scripps Institution of Oceanography, in cooperation with various worldwide groups, developed standardized methods for collecting and reporting pH data. Global ocean surveys were established, and long-term time series measuring stations were set up, including the BATS station near Bermuda and other similar stations. They consist of a series of chemical sensors, which are often launched from research vessels that make periodic trips to the regions. Improved methods for measuring pH by spectrophotometry (measuring the amount of light passing through a substance) also greatly increased the quality of measurements. Scientists ensure these measurements are valid by comparing them to measurements of related factors. These include measurements of total carbon, carbon dioxide concentration, and total alkalinity (the opposite of acidity).

In 2013, the United Nations called upon scientists to develop better techniques to measure ocean acidification. Three new techniques are expected to improve future measurements. The first are Argo floats. The floats measure sea level but also contain sensors that monitor various ocean chemistry factors, including pH. The second involves analyzing coralline algae, which are algae that have coral-like calcium deposits inside. The ratio of two isotopes of the element boron in coralline algae is determined by the pH of the water. Scientists take samples of the algae. Then, in the lab, they measure boron isotope ratios in long-lived algae and use this information to determine the pH of the water over time. Researchers from Europe and North America showed pH decline throughout the twentieth century around Alaska's Attu Island in the Bering Sea, matching rising greenhouse gas levels. The third new technique involves satellite data. Although satellites do not measure pH directly, scientists can use other satellite data—sea surface temperatures, salinity, and plankton activity—to calculate pH levels. The satellite data can be used to get a broad, spatial view of pH across the oceans.

CARBON IN THE DEPTHS

Increasing carbon dioxide concentration and decreasing pH are greatest at the ocean surface. But carbon from human sources also affects the deep ocean. In the long term, carbon at the ocean surface is transported down and mixed into deeper ocean layers. Currently, the only way to measure pH and carbon trends below the surface is by collecting repeat measurements from ships. Scientists repeat a pattern of worldwide research cruises each decade. Infrequent sampling is good enough because the deep ocean changes less from season to season and year to year than the ocean surface does. As of 2015, some ocean regions had no systematic carbon measurements and others had few. To better understand how carbon dioxide is affecting the oceans, observations need to be extended and sustained over time.

CORAL REEFS AND pH CHANGES

Coral reefs are highly diverse, productive ecosystems. They help protect coastlines from erosion, and they provide income through fisheries and tourism. They directly benefit about one-half billion people around the world who live within 60 miles (100 km) of a reef and provide goods and services worth $375 billion per year.[6] But corals, and the human communities they support, are at risk from ocean acidification. Coral skeletons are made of calcium carbonate, and increasing acidity causes the individual polyps making up corals to have difficulty creating skeletons. The reefs grow more slowly and the skeletons are more brittle and

less able to withstand stresses such as increasing water temperatures. Other marine organisms with calcium carbonate shells, such as algae, mollusks, and crustaceans, are affected in the same way.

Scientists can gather a lot of information about coral health by simply donning scuba gear, diving down into the reef, and looking at the corals. As corals grow, they produce yearly banding patterns, similar to growth rings in trees. Scientists can see banding patterns visually, but they use X-ray imaging software to see them more closely. Using a hollow, diamond-tipped drill bit, they can safely obtain small core samples from the coral. In the lab, they can analyze trapped oxygen to estimate temperature and rainfall and figure out how the climate (and the corals) have changed through time. They can determine times during the coral's history when it experienced climate extremes and expelled its algae, resulting in coral bleaching.

A marine biologist monitors bleaching on a reef.

Ocean chemistry is more affected by climate change than previously thought. Researchers from the Carnegie Institution and the University of California-Santa Cruz analyzed ocean sediment cores from 13 to 8 million years ago. Scientists drill the cores from specialized research vessels in the middle of the ocean. They use sonar to find a flat section of ocean floor. A multicore sampler holding eight sampling tubes is carefully lowered by winch, and the crew holds the ship's position steady to keep the tubes vertical. When the tubes are filled, covers automatically close over them, keeping the sample safe as it is raised to the surface. On the ship, it is quickly stored in a shipping container that keeps the temperature stable. The scientists determined that ocean calcium levels shifted significantly during the time period under study. Calcium levels are strongly tied to atmospheric carbon dioxide levels and ocean acidity. The unexpectedly dynamic nature of calcium levels suggests that ocean chemistry can change more rapidly and dramatically than previously thought. Researchers warn that the same thing could happen again as the present-day climate changes.

NEW TOOLS

Whitman Miller is a research scientist at the Smithsonian Environmental Research Center in Edgewater, Maryland. He studies how acidification affects coastal ecosystems. His research group has developed an instrument that brings air and water into equilibrium, so the air reflects the concentration of gas in the water. The water sampling part of the instrument can be fixed to the side of a dock or a boat, while the gas analyzer remains safely inside a lab on the dock or boat. After air and water samples are in equilibrium, the instrument can read ocean carbon dioxide levels from the air. Its infrared gas analyzer can be used without being soaked in water, contaminated, or affected by changes in salt levels. Miller's design is an improvement over past instruments for analyzing ocean gases because it costs less, uses updated electronic components, and is smaller.

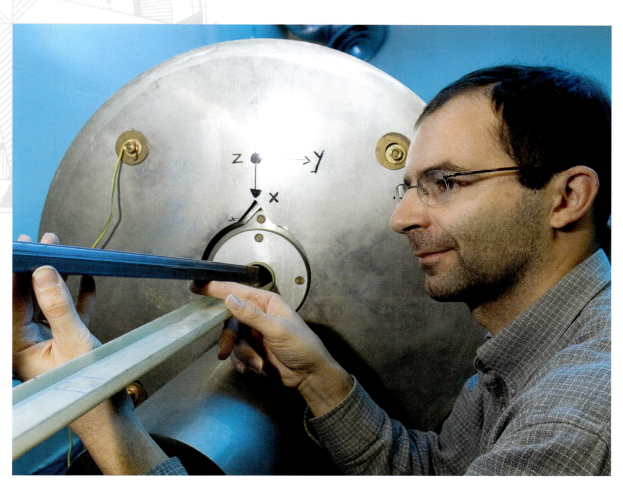

A researcher prepares to study seabed cores from the Arctic Ocean.

Ocean acidification also lowers the oceans' ability to absorb more carbon dioxide. This means more of the gas will remain in the atmosphere, further raising global temperatures. Changing ocean chemistry is poised to have serious effects on Earth's oceans in the future.

CHAPTER EIGHT

USING SATELLITE DATA

When the National Aeronautics and Space Administration (NASA) was formed in 1958, one of its tasks was developing technology for observing Earth from space. NASA designed and built the equipment, but scientific research was carried out by other agencies, especially the Weather Bureau (now NOAA) and the USGS. NASA later began research in Earth science, beginning with studies of the ozone layer in 1976. The growing recognition that Earth's climate could change rapidly, and that one cause of this change might be humans' release of greenhouse gases into the atmosphere, resulted in programs designed to observe Earth changes. These programs evolved, and in 1991 they became the Earth Observing System (EOS). As of 2018, the EOS has included 26 satellites in total that studied climate change, land use, pollution, ocean productivity, and other subjects.[1]

The European satellite ADM-Aeolus launched in 2018 and measures Earth's winds.

WHAT SATELLITES DO

Two major technological advances made weather forecasting, and then climate forecasting, possible. First was the advent of computers beginning in the 1950s, closely followed by near-Earth weather satellites in the 1960s. Since the first blurry photo was beamed from a weather satellite to Earth in 1960, photos taken by these "eyes in the skies" have become incredibly clear and detailed.[2]

Satellites have transformed weather forecasting by supplying images of weather systems around the world, observing areas that cannot be reached from the ground, and supplying vast quantities of other types of data. This makes forecasting considerably more accurate than ever before. Satellites provide information on the appearance of Earth from space, including details such as the smoke from a specific forest fire. They also provide information such as the temperature of the ocean surface and precise measurements of sea level height. A record of day-by-day and year-by-year satellite weather measurements enables scientists to build up a database describing changes in climate over the decades. This in turn provides raw material for models that can be used to predict future weather and climate.

THE EARTH OBSERVING SYSTEM

The Earth Observing System (EOS) consists of 26 satellites. The first three EOS satellites (EOS-1, 2, and 3), were launched in 1999, 2002, and 2004, and were nicknamed Terra, Aqua, and Aura. They collected data about Earth, the water cycle, and the atmosphere, respectively. As of 2019, all were still operational. Fifteen more of the total 26 are also still in orbit and collecting information.[3] EOS satellites have revolutionized the ability of scientists to monitor Earth from space and to collect data on climate change.

After the launch of the first successful weather satellite, the Television Infrared Observation Satellite (TIROS-1), in 1960, the United States began a series of seven Nimbus missions that formed the basis for modern-day weather and climate satellites. The Nimbus satellites were launched between 1964 and 1978 and provided the first consistent remote sensing of Earth. They also formed the basis for the modern era of the Global Positioning System (GPS), search and rescue, and data collection systems. A number of satellite programs followed, each with technology that improved upon previous programs and allowed for more precise data collection. Some orbit the equator and are called geostationary satellites. They are used by meteorologists in daily weather forecasts. Others orbit Earth's poles. These polar-orbiting environmental satellites produce images with much better resolution than satellites that orbit the equator. Polar-orbiting satellites provide information for many kinds of environmental applications: forecasting the weather, measuring sea and air temperatures, analyzing global plant growth, and monitoring volcanic eruptions and forest fires.

TIROS-1

On April 1, 1960, NASA launched a satellite that changed weather and climate forecasting forever. TIROS-1 lasted only 78 days, but it gave weather forecasters their first chance to see weather before it happened, potentially preventing or reducing weather disasters. It orbited from pole to pole, making it ideal for observing the entire Earth. At the time of its launch, the value of weather satellites was unproven. It became the basis for the entire fleet of weather and climate satellites that now underlie all climate research and the field of Earth system science.

Technicians work on TIROS-1.

GRACE TRACKS CLIMATE CHANGE

On May 22, 2018, NASA launched two new satellites, nicknamed GRACE-FO, for Gravity Recovery and Climate Experiment Follow-On. They are meant to replace the two GRACE satellites already in orbit, which launched in 2002 and completed their mission in 2017. Both pairs of satellites collect data on climate-based problems, including rising sea levels, melting ice sheets, and droughts. But the GRACE-FO satellites have updated equipment, including better batteries and an extra camera. Frank Webb, a project scientist at NASA's Jet Propulsion Laboratory, points out that climate change occurs over decades, not years. Thus, continuing the GRACE mission will provide data that will give scientists a better understanding of long-term trends and enable better predictions of future climate changes.

The new satellites will map changes in Earth's magnetic field, which in turn will help monitor water distribution on Earth. As the car-sized satellites orbit Earth, one 137 miles (220 km) behind the other, they use sensitive instruments to measure the exact distance between them. This data can be used to show tiny variations in Earth's gravitational pull. Long-term monitoring of these changes can show shifts in water on the ground—glaciers, snow melt, and even underground water sources. The data will improve weather models. Meteorologists will be able to better forecast catastrophic events such as droughts, floods, and water shortages. Scientists will better understand the climate. The satellites will even help predict earthquakes by detecting tiny movements in Earth's crust.

Satellite data is vital to present and future understanding of world climate. Data collected by geostationary and polar-orbiting satellites is

Geosynchronous satellites orbit around Earth's equator. Each orbit lasts 24 hours, so they stay in a fixed position over Earth. Polar satellites pass over both poles. Earth rotates beneath them, so they can view Earth's entire surface in 24 hours.

HOW SATELLITES MEASURE SEA LEVEL

NOAA manages Jason-3, a polar-orbiting satellite. Jason-3 monitors sea levels using a radar instrument called Poseidon-3B, which sends radio waves to Earth's surface and listens for their echo as they bounce off the sea. Scientists know that radio waves travel at the speed of light. Measuring the time it takes for them to travel from the satellite to the sea surface and back gives scientists the distance traveled, and therefore the sea level. Jason-3 has precise methods that correct for several factors that could decrease the accuracy of the measurement, including the satellite's exact location and the amount of moisture in the atmosphere. With these corrections, Jason-3 can measure sea level to an accuracy of less than one inch (2.5 cm) while orbiting 830 miles (1,330 km) above Earth.[4]

> "We look at this information [satellite-based climate data] as part of the national infrastructure, no different from highways and railroads and air traffic."[5]
>
> —*Waleed Abdalati, geography professor, University of Colorado–Boulder*

received by stations on the ground and archived by the NCEI. Analysts who decipher satellite data are often highly trained information technology specialists. They do many kinds of analysis. One kind involves making movies from the continuous stream of data from a single location, to show how Earth's surface changes over time. Data from five geostationary satellites can be combined to form a single image of Earth. Geostationary satellites monitor and predict events such as tropical storm systems, tornadoes, flash floods, dust storms, forest fires, and volcanic eruptions. All of this information can be used in the present to monitor and prevent catastrophes. It is also used in climate models to help predict future climate changes.

The GOES-O weather-monitoring satellite launched in 2009.

CHAPTER NINE
CLIMATE MODELING TODAY AND TOMORROW

A model is a small-scale representation of a larger system, designed to help people better understand the parts and interactions of the larger system. Smaller working versions of the real world, such as climate models, help scientists better understand a huge system that is too complex to be studied directly. Models are less detailed than the real system but larger in scope, so the modeler can see how the entire system works in a simplified state.

A climate model simulates Earth's climate. It uses a series of mathematical equations to analyze actual climate data to model past climate behavior or predict the climate in the future. The equations are based on physical, chemical, and biological laws, including the laws of thermodynamics and

Computer models of Earth help scientists understand how its large and complex systems work together.

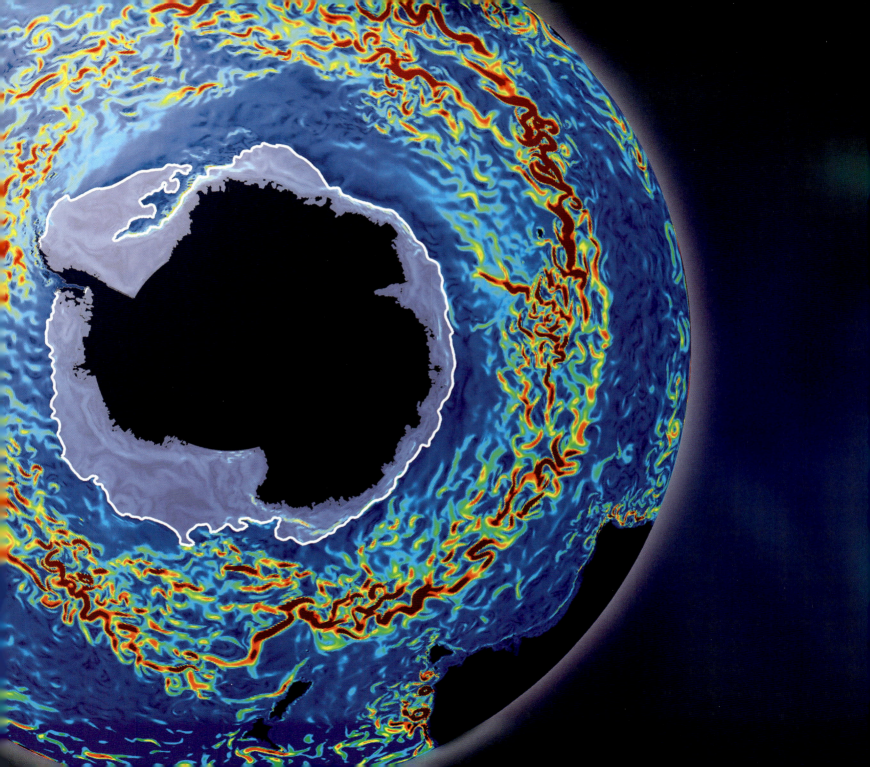

A typical global climate model is built by hundreds of people over many years, consists of 18,000 printed pages of computer code, and runs on a supercomputer as large as a tennis court.[1]

THE THEORY OF EMERGENCE

In a 2014 TED talk, Gavin Schmidt, director of the NASA Goddard Institute for Space Studies, noted that in climate models, many small interactions are programmed in, but when the model is run, larger properties will emerge that were not built in. He likens the process to choosing a sports team: the coach may choose players and tactics but cannot dictate what happens on the field. Likewise, scientists input equations describing Earth's climate plus previously collected data, and the model produces new processes—for example, ocean circulation, seasonal cycles, or flows of carbon between land and atmosphere. This illustrates the theory of emergence—the idea that something larger and more complex can come from interactions of individual pieces, or more simply, the whole is greater than the sum of its parts.

Newton's laws of motion. Data is collected from observations of temperature, precipitation, humidity, ice formation and retreat, and other factors over the years. When a good model runs on a computer, with actual climate data inserted into the equations, the result should be similar to how the climate actually behaved.

HOW CLIMATE MODELS WORK

When scientists build a climate model, they figure out which mathematical equations describe the natural laws that govern climate. These include (among many others) the first law of thermodynamics, which says energy cannot be created or destroyed, only transformed; and the Stefan-Boltzmann law, which describes Earth's greenhouse effect. They put these equations together to form a climate model—a computerized representation of how the real-world climate works. Global climate models vary, but they all have four general components: atmospheric (including clouds and wind), land surface (including vegetation, snow cover, and rivers), ocean (including current movement and mixing), and sea ice (including the heat and water exchange between sea and air).

But a model covering the entire Earth is difficult to run. All equations must be calculated for all parts of Earth. To do this, a climate model divides Earth into a three-dimensional series of grid cells, or boxes. The grid cell layers cover the height and depth of the oceans and atmosphere. The model calculates the climate within each cell, using temperature, air pressure, humidity, and wind speed within that cell. Typically, a grid cell is about 62 miles (100 km) on a side at mid-latitudes. Grid cells are smaller at the poles and larger at the equator because Earth is spherical. A higher-resolution model has smaller grid cells; it is more accurate but takes longer to run because it requires more calculations.

A climate model is run for a given time period, say a century. The modeler must decide on the time period, and on the time step, or the time between each calculation of climatic conditions. The size of the time step matters, because the climate changes continuously in the real world. As with the size of grid cells, the smaller the time step, the more realistic the model will be. The model takes information available from past and present climate, and extrapolates this information forward to the future.

THE LANGUAGE OF CLIMATE MODELING

Climate modelers usually write computer code in the programming language Fortran. This was the first computer programming language that was written in words, like a human language. Fortran was developed in the 1950s by IBM. It contains commands for the computer such as IF, THEN, ELSE, and DO. When the model is run, the computer translates the lines of Fortran code into machine code (zeros and ones) that the computer can understand.

FINDING A BALANCE

Choosing the size of the time step in a climate model requires finding a balance between accuracy and computing time. Smaller time steps increase accuracy, but require many more calculations per computer run. For example, a time step of one minute over a century would take more than 50 million calculations per grid cell, while a time step of one day during the century would require only 36,500 calculations. According to Professor Paul Williams, the best approach would be to keep decreasing the time step until the model's results stop changing. But this takes too much time and power. Williams says a time step of 30 minutes "seems to be a reasonable compromise" between accuracy and computer processing time.[4]

Climate models require huge amounts of computer power and are run on massive supercomputers. The Met Office Hadley Centre in the United Kingdom uses three Cray XC40 supercomputers. Together, they can do 14,000 trillion calculations per second.[2] In 2017, the National Center for Atmospheric Research (NCAR) in Cheyenne, Wyoming, set up a new supercomputer the size of a house. It was one of the top 20 fastest computers in the world at the time, performing 5.3 quadrillion calculations per second.[3]

TESTING AND PREDICTING

The process for testing a climate model is known as hind-casting. The model is run backward, from the present into the past. Scientists then compare the model results with observed climate conditions during that time period. Scientists test models over and over, revising their equations to increase accuracy. The more precisely they match real data, the more accurate the model is. Scientists around the world also compare their model results with each other. When many models agree, modelers gain confidence in the accuracy of their model. Once a model is shown to be accurate, it can be used to simulate future climates. Modelers then set conditions for a future

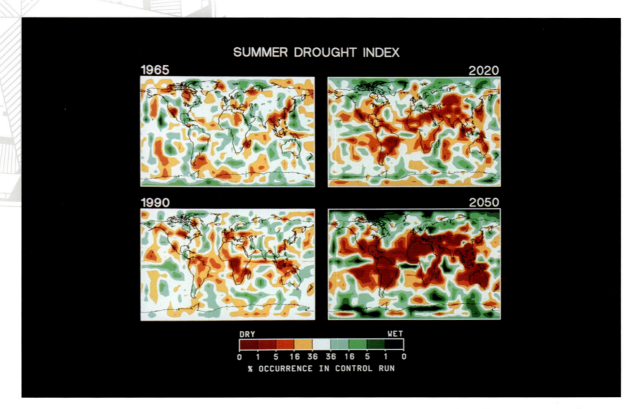

A computer model shows historical and projected summer droughts due to climate change.

climate scenario. They might consider changes in population, economics, land use, or atmospheric conditions.

Modelers can change a single feature of a climate model, such as ocean temperatures or atmospheric carbon dioxide concentrations, and determine how that change affects future climate. Or they can detect a change in the climate under a given set of conditions, determine if the change is mathematically significant, and then attempt to attribute it to a specific cause, such as a change caused by human activity.

Over the past 50 to 70 years, there has been a massive convergence of scientists cooperating to understand the problems of world climate as the dangers of global warming became obvious. Scientists of all kinds work on climate change—from computer experts building and analyzing climate models, to marine biologists diving on coral reefs, to hardy geologists braving the frozen Arctic and documenting changes in ice cover. Solving the climate crisis will require new ideas and lots of hard work. In the future, more and more scientists will be needed for this exciting—and essential—work.

Climate change touches on many fields of science. An epidemiologist who studies patterns of disease tracks how tick populations shift as climate changes.

ESSENTIAL FACTS

SIGNIFICANT EVENTS

- In the late 1950s, Caltech post-doctoral student Charles Keeling began observing atmospheric carbon dioxide levels at Mauna Loa Observatory in Hawaii.
- In 1975, Wallace Broecker published a scientific article about warming global temperatures that popularized the term "global warming."
- In 1979, satellites began tracking sea ice melt.
- In the early 1990s, Andrew Dickson of the Scripps Institution of Oceanography helped standardize how researchers collect and report ocean pH data.
- On May 22, 2018, NASA launched two new satellites, known as GRACE-FO, to collect data on sea levels, ice sheets, and droughts.
- In March 2019, carbon dioxide reached more than 414 ppm.

KEY PLAYERS

- Richard B. Alley has done decades of work on ice cores, mostly in Greenland.
- Daniel Fagre of the US Geological Survey studies melting glaciers in national parks.
- Katey M. Walter Anthony studies melting permafrost and the release of methane from frozen Arctic lakes.
- Chip Fletcher, a geologist from the University of Hawaii, studies the impact of sea level rise on Pacific islands.
- Gary Shaffer of the University of Copenhagen studies dead zones around the world.
- Paul Williams of the University of Reading is one of thousands of scientists who work on climate modeling.

IMPACT ON SCIENCE

Climate change is already affecting millions of lives. Research to better understand climate and its impact on various ecosystems and cultures will remain a top priority for decades to come. This will result in new data and potentially breakthroughs in many areas of science—physics, chemistry, biology, ecology, and more. Climate change research will continue to be a growing area.

QUOTE

"Things that normally happen in geologic time are happening during the span of a human lifetime. It's like watching the Statue of Liberty melt."

—Daniel Fagre, US Geological Survey

GLOSSARY

baseline
A value used as the starting point or the basis of calculations.

climate model
A much-simplified computer simulation of the climate, based on actual climate data and equations describing climate interactions; the model is designed to both simulate climate and predict future changes.

concentration
The proportion of a specific substance or ingredient in relation to other ingredients.

drill run
A repeating cycle of ice core sections drilled in the same hole; all the sections placed end-to-end form a complete ice core.

equilibrium
A state of being balanced.

greenhouse gas
A gas that absorbs infrared radiation and traps heat in the atmosphere.

ice core
A tube of ice removed vertically from an ice sheet or glacier, showing layers of annual ice buildup over many years and containing materials that can decode past climates.

isotope
A form of an element with a differing number of neutrons in its nucleus.

levee
A man-made embankment built to prevent water from moving into an area.

mass spectrometer
An instrument that determines the chemicals found in a substance by sorting particles by mass.

ocean acidification
Increase in acidity of the oceans resulting from increased absorption of carbon dioxide from burning fossil fuels; small increases have great effects on ocean organisms.

permafrost
Soil that has been permanently frozen for at least two years; found high in the Arctic.

thermal expansion
The increase in water volume and decrease in its density that occurs as water warms; it is one cause of sea level rise.

tide gauge
A piece of equipment that measures the height of tides, or sea level; modern tide gauges are controlled electronically by satellites.

time step
The time between two calculations of climatic conditions in a climate model.

tundra
The vast, treeless region of the Arctic where soil is permanently frozen as permafrost.

ADDITIONAL RESOURCES

SELECTED BIBLIOGRAPHY

Scripps CO2 Program. "Keeling Curve Lessons: Lessons for Long-Term Earth Observations." *Scripps Institute of Oceanography*, n.d., scrippsco2.ucsd.edu. Accessed 27 June 2019.

Treviño, Julissa. "Meet NASA's New Dynamic Duo: A Pair of Climate Change-Tracking Satellites." *Smithsonian*, 22 May 2018, smithsonianmag.com. Accessed 27 June 2019.

FURTHER READINGS

Collins, Anna. *The Climate Change Crisis*. Lucent, 2018.

Hand, Carol. *Melting Arctic Ice*. Abdo, 2018.

Lanser, Amanda. *Adapting to Climate Change*. Abdo, 2015.

ONLINE RESOURCES

To learn more about climate scientists, please visit **abdobooklinks.com** or scan this QR code. These links are routinely monitored and updated to provide the most current information available.

MORE INFORMATION

For more information on this subject, contact or visit the following organizations:

THE ARCTIC INSTITUTE
Center for Circumpolar Security Studies
PO Box 21194
Washington, DC 20009
202-350-1384
thearcticinstitute.org

The Arctic Institute does multidisciplinary research on climate change and its scientific, social, and economic effects. It forms global partnerships and writes briefs to help decision makers.

WOODS HOLE OCEANOGRAPHIC INSTITUTION
93 Water St.
Woods Hole, MA 02543
508-289-2252
whoi.edu

This nonprofit organization is dedicated to exploring and researching the ocean. It also offers many educational programs for students ranging from high school to postdoctoral. The institute has a visitor center and exhibits that showcase its work.

SOURCE NOTES

CHAPTER 1. ICE CORES AND CLIMATE CHANGE

1. Lauren Hinkel. "Big Ice, Big Science." *MIT News*, 14 Nov. 2016, news.mit.edu. Accessed 29 July 2019.

2. Richard B. Alley. *The Two-Mile Time Machine*. Princeton UP, 2000, updated preface 2014.

3. "About Ice Cores." *National Science Foundation: Ice Core Facility*, n.d., icecores.org. Accessed 29 July 2019.

4. Hinkel, "Big Ice, Big Science."

5. "About Ice Cores."

6. "About NSF-ICF." *National Science Foundation: Ice Core Facility*, n.d., icecores.org. Accessed 29 July 2019.

7. Alley, *The Two-Mile Time Machine*, 28–29.

CHAPTER 2. MELTING GLACIERS

1. Daniel Glick. "The Big Thaw." *National Geographic*, Sept. 2004, nationalgeographic.com. Accessed 29 July 2019.

2. "Graphic: Dramatic Glacier Melt." *NASA: Global Climate Change*, n.d., climate.nasa.gov. Accessed 29 July 2019.

3. Matt Williams. "What Percent of Earth Is Water?" *Phys.org*, 2 Dec. 2014, phys.org. Accessed 29 July 2019.

4. Daniel B. Fagre. "History of Glaciers in Glacier National Park." *USGS*, n.d., usgs.gov. Accessed 29 July 2019.

5. Glick, "The Big Thaw."

6. Adam Popescu. "A Greenland Glacier Is Growing. That Doesn't Mean Melting Is Over." *National Geographic*, 25 Mar. 2019, nationalgeographic.com. Accessed 29 July 2019.

7. "America's Last Remaining Glaciers." *National Park Foundation*, 14 Dec. 2015, nationalparks.org. Accessed 29 July 2019.

8. Patrick Gonzalez. "Melting Glaciers, Shifting Biomes and Dying Trees in Our National Parks." *Conversation*, 1 Sept. 2016, theconversation.com. Accessed 29 July 2019.

9. "America's Last Remaining Glaciers."

10. Erich Peitzsch and Lisa McKeon. "Retreat of Glaciers in Glacier National Park." *USGS*, n.d., usgs.gov. Accessed 29 July 2019.

11. Henry Fountain and Ben C. Solomon. "Where Glaciers Melt Away, Switzerland Sees Opportunity." *New York Times*, 14 Feb. 2018, nytimes.com. Accessed 29 July 2019.

12. "America's Last Remaining Glaciers."

13. "North Cascades National Park Washington." *National Park Service*, n.d., nps.gov. Accessed 29 July 2019.

14. Jesse Westbrook. "The Effects of Melting Glaciers on Tropical Communities." *Phys.org*, 17 Jan. 2017, phys.org. Accessed 29 July 2019.

15. Danielle Priess. "Report: Global Warming Could Melt at Least a Third of Himalayan Glaciers." *NPR*, 5 Feb. 2019, npr.org. Accessed 29 July 2019.

16. "Emissions Threaten to Melt Two-Thirds of Himalayan Glaciers." *Al Jazeera*, 4 Feb. 2019, aljazeera.com. Accessed 29 July 2019.

17. James Balog. "Why Do Glaciers Matter?" *Extreme Ice Survey*, n.d., extremeicesurvey.org. Accessed 29 July 2019.

CHAPTER 3. CARBON DIOXIDE

1. "Causes of Global Warming Explained." *National Geographic*, 17 Jan. 2019, nationalgeographic.com. Accessed 29 July 2019.

2. Rebecca Lindsey. "Climate Change: Atmospheric Carbon Dioxide." *Climate.gov*, 1 Aug. 2018, climate.gov. Accessed 29 July 2019.

3. Holly Shaftel. "10 Things: Planetary Atmospheres." *NASA Science: Solar System Exploration*, 14 May 2018, solarsystem.nasa.gov. Accessed 29 July 2019.

4. Lindsey, "Climate Change: Atmospheric Carbon Dioxide."

5. Lindsey, "Climate Change: Atmospheric Carbon Dioxide."

6. "Keeling Curve Lessons." *Scripps CO2 Program*, n.d., scrippsco2.ucsd.edu. Accessed 29 July 2019.

7. Tony Haymet and Andrew Dickson. "The Oceans' SOS." *Los Angeles Times*, 13 Dec. 2010, latimes.com. Accessed 29 July 2019.

8. Daniel Glick. "The Big Thaw." *National Geographic*, Sept. 2004, nationalgeographic.com. Accessed 29 July 2019.

9. "Daily CO2." *CO2.Earth*, 27 Mar. 2019, co2.earth. Accessed 27 Mar. 2019.

10. "Trends in Atmospheric Methane: Global CH4 Monthly Means." *Earth System Research Laboratory*, 5 July 2019, esrl.noaa.gov. Accessed 29 July 2019.

11. "Atmospheric N2O Levels Graph." *2° Institute*, n.d., n2olevels.org. Accessed 29 July 2019.

12. "Main Greenhouse Gases." *Center for Climate and Energy Solutions*, n.d., c2es.org. Accessed 29 July 2019.

CHAPTER 4. MELTING PERMAFROST

1. "Permafrost in a Warming World." *Weather Underground*, n.d., wunderground.com. Accessed 29 July 2019.

2. Laura Nielsen. "Boreholes Drilled Deep Reveal Permafrost Temperatures in Alaska." *Frontier Scientists*, 9 Aug. 2016, frontierscientists.com. Accessed 29 July 2019.

3. Justin Gillis. "As Permafrost Thaws, Scientists Study the Risks." *New York Times*, 16 Dec. 2011, nytimes.com. Accessed 29 July 2019.

4. "Permafrost in a Warming World."

5. David Grossman. "Melting Permafrost Poses a Huge Danger to Arctic Infrastructure." *Popular Mechanics*, 11 Dec. 2018, popularmechanics.com. Accessed 29 July 2019.

6. Gillis, "As Permafrost Thaws, Scientists Study the Risks."

7. Doug Criss. "Arctic Permafrost Is Melting So Fast It's Damaging the Equipment Scientists Use to Measure It." *CNN*, 6 May 2019, cnn.com. Accessed 29 July 2019.

SOURCE NOTES CONTINUED

CHAPTER 5. AT THE POLES

1. "Antarctica and Global Warming: The Effects of Global Warming on Antarctica." *Cool Antarctica*, n.d., coolantarctica.com. Accessed 29 July 2019.

2. University of Arizona. "Evolution Too Slow to Keep Up with Climate Change." *Science Daily*, 9 July 2013, sciencedaily.com. Accessed 29 July 2019.

3. Stephen Leahy. "Polar Bears Really Are Starving Because of Global Warming, Study Shows." *National Geographic*, 1 Feb. 2018, news.nationalgeographic.com. Accessed 29 July 2019.

4. Kelsey Lindsey. "How Traditional Knowledge Helps Scientists Studying Polar Bears in Greenland." *Arctic Today*, 6 June 2018, arctictoday.com. Accessed 29 July 2019.

5. Sabrina Shankman. "Arctic Sea Ice Melt, Driven by Global Warming, Accelerated by Nature." *Inside Climate News*, 14 Mar. 2017, insideclimatenews.org. Accessed 29 July 2019.

6. Joe Romm. "'Devastating' Arctic Warming of 9–16°F Now 'Locked In,' UN Researchers Warn." *ThinkProgress*, 14 Mar. 2019, thinkprogress.org. Accessed 29 July 2019.

7. "Antarctica and Global Warming."

8. Greta Moran. "What Happens in the Arctic Doesn't Stay in the Arctic." *Mother Jones*, 15 Dec. 2018, motherjones.com. Accessed 29 July 2019.

9. Katherine J. Wu. "As Climate Change Reshapes the Antarctic, These Animals Might Fall First." *NOVA*, 17 Jan. 2019, pbs.org. Accessed 29 July 2019.

10. Hugh Powell. "On the Antarctic Peninsula, Scientists Witness a Penguin Revolution." *Cornell Lab of Ornithology: All About Birds*, 26 Jan. 2016, allaboutbirds.org. Accessed 29 July 2019.

11. Jim O'Donnell. "Global Warming in Antarctica: How Climate Change Is Impacting 'The Great White Desert.'" *Zegrahm Expeditions*, 8 Mar. 2018, zegrahm.com. Accessed 29 July 2019.

12. O'Donnell, "Global Warming in Antarctica."

CHAPTER 6. RISING SEA LEVELS

1. Christina Nunez. "Sea Level Rise, Explained." *National Geographic*, n.d., nationalgeographic.com. Accessed 29 July 2019.

2. Amy Braunschweiger. "Interview: Climate Change and the Disappearing Islands of Kiribati." *Human Rights Watch*, 15 June 2018, hrw.org. Accessed 29 July 2019.

3. "Current Status of Argo." *About Argo*, n.d., argo.ucsd.edu. Accessed 29 July 2019.

4. Richard Schiffman. "As Seas Rise, Tropical Pacific Islands Face a Perfect Storm." *Yale Environment 360*, 6 July 2017, e360.yale.edu. Accessed 29 July 2019.

5. Simon Albert et al. "Sea Level Rise Swallows 5 Whole Pacific Islands." *Scientific American*, 9 May 2016, scientificamerican.com. Accessed 29 July 2019.

6. Alice Klein. "Eight Low-Lying Pacific Islands Swallowed Whole by Rising Seas." *New Scientist*, 7 Sept. 2017, newscientist.com. Accessed 29 July 2019.

7. Nunez, "Sea Level Rise, Explained."

8. Rosanna Xia. "Destruction from Sea Level Rise in California Could Exceed Worst Wildfires and Earthquakes, New Research Shows." *Los Angeles Times*, 13 Mar. 2019, latimes.com. Accessed 29 July 2019.

CHAPTER 7. OCEAN CHEMISTRY

1. "Global Warming's Evil Twin: Ocean Acidification." *Climate Reality Project*, 21 June 2016, climaterealityproject.org. Accessed 29 July 2019.

2. Toste Tanhua et al. "Monitoring Ocean Carbon and Ocean Acidification." *World Meteorological Association*, 2015, public.wmo.int. Accessed 29 July 2019.

3. Brian Merchant. "By 2100, Earth Will Have an Entirely Different Ocean." *Vice*, 13 Aug. 2015, motherboard.vice.com. Accessed 29 July 2019.

4. Merchant, "By 2100, Earth Will Have an Entirely Different Ocean."

5. Merchant, "By 2100, Earth Will Have an Entirely Different Ocean."

6. "Global Warming's Evil Twin."

CHAPTER 8. USING SATELLITE DATA

1. Nola Taylor Redd. "Earth Observing System: Monitoring the Planet's Climate." *Space*, 1 Feb. 2018, space.com. Accessed 29 July 2019.

2. Fedor Kossakovski. "How Do Satellites Track Weather and Climate Change?" *Miles O'Brien Productions*, 19 Jan. 2018, milesobrien.com. Accessed 29 July 2019.

3. Redd, "Earth Observing System: Monitoring the Planet's Climate."

4. Kossakovski, "How Do Satellites Track Weather and Climate Change?"

5. Francie Diep. "The Future of America's Satellites." *Pacific Standard*, 9 Jan. 2018, psmag.com. Accessed 29 July 2019.

CHAPTER 9. CLIMATE MODELING TODAY AND TOMORROW

1. "Q&A: How Do Climate Models Work?" *Carbon Brief*, 15 Jan. 2018, carbonbrief.org. Accessed 29 July 2019.

2. "Q&A: How Do Climate Models Work?"

3. Bill Mannel. "Supercomputers Helping Researchers Predict Climate Change." *HPCwire*, 15 May 2017, hpcwire.com. Accessed 29 July 2019.

4. "Q&A: How Do Climate Models Work?"

INDEX

aerial photography, 20, 43
Alaska, 14, 18, 20, 27, 36, 39–40, 44, 45, 53, 79
algae, 53, 54, 76, 78–79, 81
Alley, Richard, 4–6, 7, 13
Andes Mountains, 21
Antarctica, 9, 10, 46, 53–57, 72
Arctic cultures, 27, 46, 53
Argo floats, 64, 78
art installations, 62

Bates, Nicholas, 31
Bermuda Atlantic Time-series Study (BATS) station, 31, 78
Bikini Atoll, 7
Boes, Robert, 20
Broecker, Wallace, 31
Brower, Eugene, 27

Cable, William, 39
calcium, 78–82
carbon dioxide
    air sampling, 27–28, 31–32
    atmospheric levels, 6, 13, 24, 26–28, 32, 34, 82, 97
    ocean absorption, 74, 79, 82–83
    ocean sampling, 29–31, 78, 79
    release of, 38, 39, 40, 44, 45, 76
    temperature, effect on, 26–27
carbon sink, 40, 74
carbonic acid, 74
climate change refugees, 69, 71
Climate Variability and Predictability Experiment (CLIVAR), 64
computer models, 13, 21, 44, 45, 49, 51, 66, 67, 71, 76, 86, 89, 90, 92–98
    grid cells, 95, 96
    hind-casting, 96
    time steps, 95–96
coral reefs, 16, 67, 76, 79–81, 98

dead zone, 76
deforestation, 18, 27
Dickson, Andrew, 28, 78
Ding, Qinghua, 51

economic activities, 16–17, 20–22, 27, 44–45, 53, 67–71
emergence, theory of, 94
erosion, 27, 53, 60, 62, 66–67, 71, 79
evolution rates, 48

Fagre, Daniel, 14, 16
feedback loops, 38, 39, 45, 46, 48, 57
Fitzpatrick, Joan, 4
Fletcher, Chip, 64–66, 67
flooding, 16–17, 22, 53, 60, 66, 67, 69–71, 89, 90
freshwater, 16–17, 60, 66

Glacier National Park, 14–16, 18–20
glaciers
    formation, 14, 16
    measurements, 18, 20, 89
    retreat, 14–22, 57, 72
global warming potential (GWP), 34
Gonzalez, Patrick, 17–18
greenhouse effect, 24–26, 94
Greenland, 4–10, 16, 49, 51, 72
Grosse, Guido, 40

habitat loss, 17, 48–49, 53–54, 60
Hansen, Brage Bremset, 49–51
Hindu Kush Himalayan (HKH) region, 21
hydropower, 17, 20
Hydrostation S, 29–31

ice cores
    analysis, 6–7, 10–13
    drilling, 4–6, 7–9, 10, 13, 58
ice sheets, 4, 7–9, 10, 16, 46, 51, 53, 57, 72, 88
Indonesia, 69
Industrial Revolution, 6, 26, 40, 74, 76
infrared gas analyzers, 28, 82
infrastructure, 27, 38, 44–45
islands disappearing, 16, 66–69, 71
isotopes, 6–7, 28, 78–79

Jacobshavn Glacier, 16

Keeling, Charles David, 27–28, 32
Keeling curve, 28, 32
Kiribati, 62, 67, 69
krill, 54–57

Laidre, Kristen, 49

Mark, Bryan, 21
Mars, 26
Marshall Islands, 64, 67
mass spectrometer, 7
Mauna Loa Observatory, 28
methane, 6, 24, 26, 32, 34, 38–43, 45, 48
Micronesia, 67
Miller, Whitman, 82
Morley, Simon, 53–54
Muir Glacier, 14
Multidisciplinary drifting Observatory for the Study of Arctic Climate (MOSAiC) expedition, 58

National Science Foundation Ice Core Facility (NSF-ICF), 10
Netherlands, 69–70
nitrous oxide, 24, 32, 34
Nunn, Patrick, 67–69

ocean acidity, 74–79, 82–83
ocean currents, 29, 31, 64, 95
ocean sediment cores, 82
ocean temperature, 16, 31, 64, 72, 76, 79, 81, 86, 87, 97
Osterkamp, Tom, 39

peat, 40
penguins, 54
permafrost, 13, 27, 36–45, 48, 53
pH monitoring, 76–79
plankton, 53, 79
polar amplification, 48
polar bears, 48–49, 53, 58

Quintero, Ignacio, 48

radiocarbon dating, 67
reindeer, 49–51

Samoa, 64, 67
satellites, 13, 20, 43, 44, 51, 64, 67, 79, 84–90
  altimetry, 63
  Earth Observing System (EOS), 84, 86
  geostationary, 87, 89–90
  Geostationary Operational Environmental Satellite (GOES), 62
  Gravity Recovery and Climate Experiment Follow-On (GRACE-FO), 88
  Jason, 64, 89
  polar-orbiting, 87, 89
  TIROS-1, 87
Schmidt, Gavin, 94
sea ice, 27, 46, 48, 49, 51–54, 58, 72, 95
Sea Level Fine Resolution Acoustic Measuring Equipment (SEAFRAME), 64

sea level rise
  causes, 16, 22, 51, 72
  effects, 16, 60, 66–71
  measurements, 18, 62–64, 78, 86, 88, 89
Shaffer, Gary, 76
Siberia, 39–40, 58
Small Island Developing States (SIDS), 67
Solomon Islands, 67
spectrophotometry, 78
Sperry Glacier, 14
Stommel, Henry, 29
supercomputers, 94, 96

Takahashi, Taro, 76
Tans, Pieter, 32
thermal expansion, 72
tidal gauges, 18, 62–64
tundra, 40
Turetsky, Merritt, 45

Venus, 26

Walter Anthony, Katey M., 39–43
water shortages, 17, 22, 66–67, 89
Webb, Frank, 88
Webster, Melinda, 58
whales, 54
Wiens, John, 48
Williams, Paul, 96
Willis, Josh, 16

Zimmerer, Karl, 21

ABOUT THE AUTHOR

Carol Hand has a PhD in zoology with a specialization in marine ecology and a special interest in environmental problems and climate science. Before becoming a science writer, she taught college, wrote for standardized testing companies, and developed multimedia science curricula. She has written more than 60 books for young people on topics including glaciers and climate change.